T0371804

Preface

I'VE BEEN MAKING OR HELPING TO MAKE YOGURT since I was about ten years old, and according to my mom, eating copious amounts of it since I was able to hold a spoon. I grew up eating Greek yogurt, but being part Greek, to us it was just yogurt. Our homemade yogurt, made from the milk of our golden Guernsey cow Buttercup, was strained through a draining box my father had fashioned. My mother would drape a finely woven muslin cloth over the box and then secure it with a wire, which tucked into a groove about 1 inch from the top of the box. The rich yogurt was then poured into the cloth and covered while the whey exited from little tunnels at the bottom of the box onto a drain board and into the sink. My favorite way to eat yogurt back then was (and it is still a guilty pleasure) to deposit a large spoonful of thick, raw local honey on top of the chilled yogurt and then use the same spoon to eat it, scraping the extra honey from the spoon a little bit at time.

It wasn't until I was a teenager that I ate my first commercially made yogurt. I bought a container at the local market and used a spoon from the deli to give it a try. It was sweet, custardy, and mild, and I didn't know that I was supposed to stir up the fruit on the bottom. Being a teen with the typical sweet tooth, I loved it, but to me it wasn't real yogurt — plain, fresh, and with nuances of flavor.

For almost all of my adult years I have made yogurt for my family, mostly from store-purchased milk and later from our own goat's milk. It's always been for a trifecta of reasons: to save money, to reduce plastic waste, and (the best reason) for the flavor! Because I grew up making yogurt and have been doing it for so long (close to 40 years now if we're counting), I had always thought that yogurt making was simple. As I explored the greater world of dairy ferments, it became obvious that not only can the process become complicated, but there is a world of surprising, almost unknown milk ferments out there waiting to be explored. My goal in writing this book is not only to open up the possibilities and enhance the enjoyment and success of making these products but also to share ways to work them into meals that preserve their amazing probiotic health benefits. I hope you enjoy!

the magic of
fermented milk

homemade
yogurt
&kefir

homemade
yogurt
&kefir

71 Recipes for Making & Using Probiotic-Rich Ferments
Gianaclis Caldwell

photography by carmen troesser

Storey Publishing

For my mom, who fed me that first spoonful of yogurt so long ago
and has nurtured and inspired my path in so many ways since

*The mission of Storey Publishing is to serve our customers by
publishing practical information that encourages
personal independence in harmony with the environment.*

EDITED BY Carleen Madigan and Sarah Guare
ART DIRECTION AND BOOK DESIGN BY Carolyn Eckert
TEXT PRODUCTION BY Jennifer Jepson Smith
INDEXED BY Christine R. Lindemer, Boston Road
    Communications

COVER PHOTOGRAPHY BY © Carmen Troesser, except
    Mars Vilaubi, spine
INTERIOR PHOTOGRAPHY BY © Carmen Troesser
ADDITIONAL PHOTOGRAPHY BY Mars Vilaubi, 81 and
    throughout; courtesy of Bellwether Farms, 63;
    courtesy of Redwood Hill Farm & Creamery, 22 & 23
ORNAMENT BACKGROUNDS AND BORDERS page 1
    and throughout, Owen Jones, *Examples of Chinese
    Ornament*, 1867, collection of the Metropolitan
    Museum of Art, New York/Wikimedia Commons
PHOTO STYLING BY Carmen Troesser
FOOD STYLING BY Gianaclis Caldwell
MAP ILLUSTRATION by Ilona Sherratt, page 13

TEXT © 2020 by Gianaclis Caldwell

Storey Publishing
210 MASS MoCA Way
North Adams, MA 01247
storey.com

Printed in China through Asia Pacific Offset on paper
from responsible sources
10 9 8 7 6 5 4 3 2

LIBRARY OF CONGRESS CATALOGING-IN-
PUBLICATION DATA ON FILE

All rights reserved. Hachette Book Group supports
the right to free expression and the value of copyright.
The purpose of copyright is to encourage writers and
artists to produce the creative works that enrich our
culture. The scanning, uploading, and distribution of
this book without permission is a theft of the author's
intellectual property. If you would like permission to
use material from the book (other than for review
purposes), please contact permissions@hbgusa.com.
Thank you for your support of the author's rights.

The information in this book is true and complete
to the best of our knowledge. All recommendations
are made without guarantee on the part of the author
or Storey Publishing. The author and publisher
disclaim any liability in connection with the use of this
information.

The publisher is not responsible for websites (or
their content) that are not owned by the publisher.

Storey books may be purchased in bulk for
business, educational, or promotional use.
Special editions or book excerpts can also be
created to specification. For details, please
contact your local bookseller or the Hachette
Book Group Special Markets Department at
special.markets@hbgusa.com.

This publication is intended to provide educational information for the reader on the covered
subject. It is not intended to take the place of
personalized medical counseling, diagnosis, and
treatment from a trained health professional.
Be sure to read all instructions thoroughly before
using any of the techniques or recipes in this
book and follow all safety guidelines.

Contents

FERMENTED MILK helps support what is arguably the most important system in our bodies: our microbiome — the unseen fungi, viruses, and bacteria whose population exceeds that of our own body cells. A healthy microbiome is essential for a healthy body.

If we could study our daily world through the lens of a high-powered microscope, we might be a bit disconcerted to find that even when solitary, we are not alone. Our skin, the air surrounding us, and virtually every surface in our environment is teeming with tiny life-forms. Bacteria, viruses, molds, and yeasts inhabit all but the most recently steril-ized environments. Rather than think of these microorganisms as "germs" and contami-nants, we should see them for what they truly are: essential parts of the planet and all life on it. Fortunately, we live in a time when science and popular wisdom are embracing the role that microbes play in our lives and health. Indeed, it's now easier than ever to find foods that have been customized for us by the best nutritionists ever — fermentation microbes.

Fermented, probiotic dairy products are among the best "functional foods" — that is, foods that promote health beyond providing basic nutrition. This is thanks to the probiotic microbes they contain, which produce a wide range of by-products and benefits that trans-form already nutritious milk into something approaching a superfood. The word *probiotic* literally translates to "for life." The World Health Organization (WHO) defines *probiotics* as "microorganisms that when administered in an adequate amount confer a beneficial health effect on the host." They work with and support the human microbiome. Here are the known functions of probiotic microbes:

- They inhabit and coat the lining of the intestinal tract, leaving little room for pathogens to attach.
- They provide surface area that tricks pathogens into attaching to them rather than to our intestinal lining.
- They produce acid that keeps the intestinal tract more acidic — a condition that most pathogens don't do well in.
- They produce bacteriocins (natural antimicrobials) that target pathogens for destruction.
- They work as an immune system thermo-stat, increasing immune activity during an infection and decreasing it during anti-inflammatory, autoimmune, and allergy conditions.
- Probiotic yeasts can survive antibiotic therapy, helping the patient during such treatment.

Regular consumption of probiotics and prebiotics (nutrients that the probiotic bacteria need to survive, like fiber) nurtures a healthy gut and microbiome. The effects of fermented milk probiotics on gastrointestinal problems such as digestive dysfunction, infectious diarrhea, antibiotic-associated diarrhea, gastroenteritis, and vaginal flora insufficiency have all been well studied. Fermented milk probiotics are also being studied for uses in maintaining a healthy weight, controlling blood pressure, preventing cancer, treating the gastric–ulcer associated bacterium *Helicobacter pylori*, and even enhancing mood.

All fermented milk probiotics are not created equal, however! Different products have different amounts and types of microbes, which influence each product's nutritional value. Each culture (the source of fermenting microbes), whether it's a commercially produced culture (the most understood, or defined), a 100-year-old heirloom culture, or a lively glob of kefir grains (with the broadest spectrum of microbes), might offer a different array of microbes, from those that are primarily probiotic to those that simply do the fermentation work. Plus, it's truly impossible to quantify the numbers of live, active microbes in a jar of yogurt, especially since the number decreases the longer it sits in your fridge. Just remember that the fresher a fermented milk product is, the more microbes will be alive and well — and available for your body's benefit.

I gathered the recipes in part 3 of this book with microbes in mind, so that you can get the full benefit of these probiotic bacteria. These dishes are meant to be consumed cold or at room temperature because heat will destroy many of the most beneficial bacteria. You can certainly use yogurt and other fermented milk products in many other ways, such as in hot curries and gravies or on your steaming-hot baked potato, but with heat, the probiotic benefits are likely to be lost. And remember, you can also use purchased dairy ferments to make any of the recipes in part 3!

part one

HISTORY, TOOLS, AND TECHNIQUES OF MILK FERMENTATION

chapter 1

In the Beginning, There Was Milk

People have been eating yogurt and its kin for as long as they've been milking dairy animals. Milk ferments (like most fermented products) were probably discovered by accident when people left milk sitting in a vessel on a warm day. Although we'll never know what, or if, our earliest forebears named their primordial batches of fermented milk, we do know that they enjoyed it and kept

making more! This tangy curd is one of humanity's oldest "manufactured" foods, and it was a staple source of nutrition for those same early farmers who first began growing grain in the region we have come to think of as the birthplace of civilization: the Fertile Crescent.

The First Fermenters

Extending along the northeastern edges of the Mediterranean Sea is the Anatolian peninsula, better known today as the country of Turkey. Just down the eastern coast you'll find the nations of Syria, Lebanon, and Israel, and even farther toward the rising sun, Iraq and Iran. It was here, in this wide swath of the planet historically known as the Fertile Crescent, that farming first took root. The cultivation of grain eventually gave rise to rustic sourdough bread and robust, albeit low-alcohol, beer. The grain that made these delights possible also made it possible to domesticate and feed livestock — and subsequently, to obtain a supply of nutritious milk.

Goats and sheep are ideally suited to the native forages, weather, and topography of this part of the world. Over time, wild herds were tamed and bred, and they became mankind's first farm animals. No one is quite sure when humans began to milk these animals, but it's clear from residues on clay artifacts that fermented dairy products were part of the Neolithic diet by at least 8000 BCE. It's easy to imagine that dairy might have been a part of our ancestors' diet even earlier than that, but it was collected in vessels that didn't survive the travails of time — such as animal skins and tightly woven baskets — providing no evidence for archaeologists to discover.

Once humans began harvesting milk, it would have been impossible for them to prevent the milk from naturally fermenting into a thickened, slightly sour product quite similar to our modern drinkable yogurt, buttermilk, and kefir. The myriad wild bacteria and yeasts on the animal's teats, in the air, and embedded

The Fertile Crescent and surrounding regions (highlighted in yellow below) are considered the birthplace of fermented dairy.

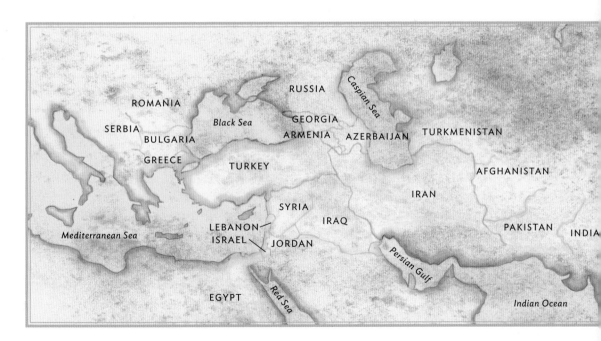

in the surface of containers would have ensured this spontaneous transformation. Different microbes would have been favored depending on the temperature of the day. The cooler the day, the more likely something like kefir and buttermilk would have formed. The hotter the day, the more likely that bacteria related to our modern yogurt cultures would have thrived. It's no coincidence that yogurt was perfected in the warmest regions of eastern Europe and Asia! Over time and reuse, the fermentation vessels themselves would have become a source of a consistent supply of helpful microbes that eagerly devoured the milk sugars and converted the milk into delicious, healthy, fermented products. Author Anne Mendelson, in her magnificent book *Milk: The Surprising Story of Milk through the Ages*, coined the wonderful term "Yogurtistan" to describe the contiguous portions of the Mediterranean, Europe, and Asia in which yogurt, kefir, and koumiss (fermented mare's milk) became cherished staples.

The Lactose Paradox

The first dairy farmers had a complicated relationship with milk. After early childhood they, like 65 to 75 percent of the population today, were unable to completely digest the milk sugar lactose. When we are infants and deriving all our nourishment from breast milk, our stomachs provide an enzyme, called lactase, that breaks the lactose molecule into two simple sugars: glucose and galactose. These simple sugars are very easy for our bodies to digest. After weaning, most of us lose the ability to produce this enzyme — a situation properly called lactase nonpersistence but known more commonly as lactose intolerance — as did all of our early ancestors.

Just under 8,000 years ago, some humans started to maintain the ability to produce lactase as adults (called lactase persistence). Surprisingly, it wasn't our Yogurtistan forebears who developed this ability but farmers farther to the north, where the days and growing season are shorter. This genetic mutation quickly spread, in evolutionary terms, through the regional population. There are various theories as to why, but the consensus is that it took a tremendous amount of genetic pressure for tolerance to develop — in other words, those who were able to digest fresh milk were also more likely to survive and thrive in the northern latitudes.

For the people today who can't easily process that pesky lactose molecule, the good news is that fermentation reduces its content in milk. While the milk ferments, lactic acid bacteria (LAB) convert lactose, through several steps, into lactic acid and some other by-products. The longer the milk ferments, the less lactose remains in the milk (until the milk reaches a level of acidity that inhibits microbial growth). If the thickened, soured milk is subsequently drained, even more lactose is removed. This would help explain why fermented milk products were first developed in regions where most people historically were, and are today, lactose intolerant.

But wait, there's more! Once you've finished your cup of yogurt or glass of kefir, your digestive system destroys many of the fermentation bacteria and releases more sugar-busting enzymes that are capable of breaking down some of the remaining lactose in your gut. Depending on your degree of lactose intolerance, your body may be able to easily digest fermented dairy products and so fully utilize their health benefits.

What's in a Name?

Yogurt has gone by many names over its long history of popularity (see the chart at right), but the Turkish words *yoğurmak* and *jugurt*, meaning "to thicken" or "to curdle," are cited as being the likely source of the most popular word now used — yogurt. Yogurt makes an appearance in the writings of Pliny the Elder (that often-quoted Roman author and naturalist) in 100 BCE and in Turkish books written in the eleventh century, where yogurt is described as a treatment for various health maladies. It is reputed to have been a mainstay in the diet of Genghis Khan, and it is said to have been brought to France by King Francis I in 1542. Its widespread use throughout Europe, the Middle East, and Asia is evidenced by the myriad names by which it was, and often still is, known.

The origin of the word *kefir* remains as mysterious as the origin of the gelatinous clusters of kefir microbes, called grains, themselves. Some people cite Turkish roots that mean "long life" and "good life"; others say it comes from the Old Turkic (a large group of languages from Asia and Eurasia) word *köpür*, meaning "froth" or "foam." A Russian website I visited claims it means "pleasure drink." One thing that is agreed upon is that people from the Caucasus region, between the Black Sea and the Caspian Sea, have been drinking kefir for a long time. Purportedly, the grains were considered a gift from the prophet Muhammad and were highly valued family treasures not to be shared with outsiders. A movie-worthy tale involving a beautiful young woman, espionage, and a kidnapping explains the true story of how kefir grains were brought out of seclusion and into the modern market in the early 1900s in Russia (see page 16 for the full story).

A Sampling of Yogurt Names from around the World

NATION	NAMES FOR YOGURT
Turkey	Jugurt, yoğurmak
Greece	Yiaourti
Georgia, Armenia, Azerbaijan	Katyk, madzoon, matsoni
Russia	Donskaya, guslyanka, kurugna, ryzhenka, varenetes
Lebanon	Laban, leban
Egypt and Sudan	Zabady
Iran and Afghanistan	Doogh, mast
Iraq	Roba
India and Pakistan	Dadhi, dahi
Mongolia	Tarag
Nepal	Sho, shosim, thara
Finland	Viili
Scandinavia	Fillbunke, filmjölk, long-mjolk, sumelk, taettem
Iceland	Skyr
Portugal	Iogurte
France	Yaourt
English-speaking countries	Yoghurt, yogurt

How Kefir Came to Russia

Kefir has been adored for its medicinal value for hundreds of years. The following story is excerpted with permission from the Yemoos Nourishing Cultures website (see Resources).

Kefir was largely unknown outside the Caucasus until the end of the nineteenth century, when news spread of studies documenting its effectiveness as a treatment for tuberculosis and for intestinal and stomach diseases. However, kefir was extremely difficult to obtain, and commercial production was not possible without first obtaining a source of grains.

Members of the All-Russian Physicians Society were determined to obtain kefir grains in order to make kefir readily available to their patients. In the early 1900s, a representative of the society approached two brothers by the name of Blandov and asked them to procure some kefir grains. The Blandovs owned and ran the Moscow Dairy, but they also had holdings in the Caucasus Mountains area, including cheese manufacturing factories in the town of Kislovodsk. The plan was for the Blandovs to obtain a source of kefir grains and then produce kefir on an industrial scale in Moscow.

The Blandovs were excited, since they knew that they would be the only commercial producers of this much-sought-after product. Nikolai Blandov sent a beautiful young employee, Irina Sakharova, to the court of a local prince, Bek-Mirza Barchorov, to charm the prince and persuade him to give her some of his kefir grains.

Unfortunately, everything did not go according to plan. The prince was very taken with the young Irina and didn't want to lose her. However, fearing retribution for violating a religious law, he had no intention of giving away any "Grains of the Prophet." Realizing that they were not going to complete their mission, Irina and her party departed for Kislovodsk. On their way home, they were stopped by mountain tribesmen, who kidnapped Irina and took her back to the prince. Since it was a local custom to steal a bride, Irina was told that she was to marry Bek-Mirza Barchorov. Only a daring rescue mission mounted by agents of her employers saved Irina from the forced marriage. The unlucky prince was brought before the tsar, who ruled that the prince was to give Irina 10 pounds of kefir grains as recompense for the insults she had endured.

The kefir grains were taken to the Moscow Dairy, and in September 1908, the first bottles of kefir drink were offered for sale in Moscow. Small quantities of kefir were produced in several small towns in the area, where there was a ready market for it. People mostly consumed it for its alleged medicinal value.

Commercial manufacturing of kefir on a large scale began in Russia in the 1930s. In 1973, the Soviet Union's minister of the food industry sent a letter to Irina Sakharova thanking her for bringing kefir to the Russian people.

The Rise of Yogurt and Yogurtlike Ferments

Yogurt began its rise to its current fame in the early 1900s, when Elie Metchnikoff (or Ilya Mechnikov), a Russian scientist and Nobel laureate, concluded that the good health and longevity of the Bulgarian people could be attributed to the presence of *Lactobacillus bulgaricus* in the yogurt that was a staple food in their diets. This species of bacteria had been discovered just a few years earlier by a Bulgarian medical student, Stamen Grigorov. Metchnikoff proposed that a diet containing these lactobacilli could ward off the ill effects of pathogenic microorganisms in the gut.

In the early twentieth century, Isaac Curasso and his family fled the Balkan Wars in what is now a part of Greece and moved to Spain. Curasso was familiar with Metchnikoff's ideas about the lactobacilli found in yogurt. In Barcelona, he saw that many children suffered from intestinal infections, and he believed that yogurt — a Balkan staple — could help them. In 1919 he opened a small business selling yogurt. He named it Danone after his son, Daniel. In 1929 Daniel Curasso opened a yogurt plant in France. (That same year, Colombo Yogurt, founded by Armenian immigrants Rose and Sarkis Colombosian, went into production in Andover, Massachusetts.) A few years later, threats of Nazi persecution forced the Curasso family out of France and to North America, where in 1941 they opened the company still known today as Dannon Yogurt.

For the first few years, Dannon struggled to survive. Then, in the late 1940s, Daniel's partner, Juan Metzger, made a brilliant marketing decision — add a dollop of jam to the bottom of each cup. Fruit-at-the-bottom yogurt was born and the company prospered. (For a highlights reel of the history of yogurt, check out the timeline on page 217.)

There's a good reason why jam made yogurt a financial success: humans are hardwired to love the taste of sugar. We are genetically designed to crave quick-energy foods in order to survive. However, the vast supply of sugar that is readily available today has outpaced our bodies' evolution, common sense, and ability to self-regulate. The modern grocery store is the creation of over 100 years of marketing trends, growth, and competition. It is filled with food products designed to taste better, look better, and, most importantly, sell better than any of their competition. Added sugar, reduced fat, extra thickeners, flavor enhancers, artificial colors, new gimmicks — you name it, yogurt has been subjected to it. (Kefir, being the new ferment in town, has yet to see the same degree of interference, but you can bet it's coming.)

Meanwhile in other parts of the world, including the original Yogurtistan regions, yogurt and yogurtlike ferments began to take on unique regional characteristics — some created by those doing the ferments and others through the influence of naturally present microbes. The most viscous, gelatinous yogurt possible, viili (page 111), evolved in Scandinavia and has been recultured and passed down through the generations. In Russia and parts of eastern Europe, a practice developed of baking milk until it has a dark, rich brown color and caramel flavor and then culturing it, often with a crust of mottled milk skin on top, to create ryazhenka (page 79). In

Vietnam, yogurt is made with a combination of sweetened condensed milk and high-heat-treated milk (page 82).

If you visit a typical American grocery store, you will likely find a yogurt section that occupies at least 12 feet of aisle space. (My local Kroger-owned store has a whopping 24 feet of conventional space allocated to yogurts and kefirs, plus 12 feet of "natural and alternative" versions. I had planned on counting the number of brands and flavors, but I didn't have enough time to do it!) You might not find a single container of plain whole-milk yogurt, and even if you do, it will likely have added thickeners such as nonfat milk powder, guar gum, or carrageenan.

What started out as the ultimate health food is now often a highly processed product with enough sugar to qualify as dessert. You could argue that the probiotics are canceled out by the added sugar, as gut bacteria do not thrive on a high-sugar diet.

When you make your own yogurt, you can avoid all that unnecessary sugar and unwanted additives. You can also use the milk of your choice and — as a bonus to the planet — reduce packaging waste. Furthermore, you can make the healthiest, most pure, most delicious yogurt for a fraction of the cost of the high-end versions you'll find at specialty grocery stores. The same holds true for all the other dairy ferments we'll talk about in this book. When it comes to health, flavor, cost, and ecological benefits, homemade reigns supreme.

The Lactobacillus bulgaricus *Debate*

The yogurt bacteria named in honor of those long-lived Bulgarians, *Lactobacillus delbrueckii* subspecies *bulgaricus* (abbreviated *L.* or *Lb. bulgaricus*), was originally thought to be responsible for the health and longevity of yogurt eaters. Over the century since its identification, however, there has been great debate as to whether or not it fits the definition of a probiotic bacterium. As recently as 2005, two studies were published with the opposite results! One study found it to be a probiotic, and the other did not.

The question may be one of definition. When broken down by bile acids in the small intestine, both *Lb. bulgaricus* and its yogurt fermentation partner *Streptococcus thermophilus* release lactase, the enzyme that breaks down lactose. By some definitions, their assistance in digestion means that these microbes are probiotic. However, some studies have shown that they don't survive passage through the gut (another way that probiotics are currently defined).

Suffice it to say that the debate goes on, and you can expect to see both of these microbes labeled in one way or the other for some time. Only time will tell if scientist Elie Metchnikoff was correct.

chapter 2

All about Milk and Microbes

The two main components of the ferments in this book are milk (dairy or plant) and microbial cultures. To the purist, the term *milk* applies only to the secretions of the mammary gland, but many food companies and consumers also call whitish liquids extracted from plants — such as coconuts and soybeans — milk. In this book, if the source of the milk isn't a mammary gland, I'll define the provenance, such as *almond* milk, and in no situation will I use the term *dairy* to describe a product derived from a field of soybeans or a coconut grove.

All milk seems to be the same at first glance — white, liquid, and available at every corner market and gas station in the United States — but practice and research tell us that not all milks are created equal. Milk ferments are only as good as the milk used to make them.

Dairy Milk

The best milk for fermentation comes straight from the animal and is never chilled, homogenized, packaged, or transported. One of my favorite truisms is "milk was never designed to see the light of day." In other words, nature designed milk to go straight from the mother's teat into the mouth and then the stomach of her infant, where it is immediately acidified and curdled. Each step we add in our attempt to preserve milk as a drinking liquid decreases its quality and character. The closest you can come to mimicking nature is to take the milk from the animal and immediately ferment it into yogurt, kefir, or cheese — much like the young mammal's own stomach would do.

The most common sources for dairy milk are cows and goats. Sheep's milk is rarely available for purchase but of course can be produced at home, and water buffalo milk is even harder to find — as are water buffaloes! Even if you don't get a chance to make your own dairy ferments from sheep or water buffalo milk, it's definitely worth sampling commercial varieties when you find them. Each type of milk has its own peculiarities when it comes to selecting and working with it.

COW'S MILK is the most common type of dairy milk in the Western Hemisphere; cows definitely hold the title of dairy queen when it comes to the volume of milk produced and used. You'll have many choices when it comes to choosing cow's milk (more on that in Keeping It Fresh on page 21), but one of the most unique differences is the characteristic of "creaming" — when the fat globules cluster together and rise to the top. When using whole, nonhomogenized milk for dairy ferments, you'll end up with a luscious, heavy layer of cream on top. Milk from pasture-reaised cows is also typically more yellow because the beta-carotene cows eat when grazing on healthy pastures lends its red-orange pigment to the milk. (Our bodies convert beta-carotene into vitamin A.) Goats, sheep, and water buffalo convert beta-carotene into vitamin A before it becomes a part of the milk, making their milk much snowier in hue.

GOAT'S MILK fat is very delicate and prone to damage that quickly alters the flavor of the milk and can make it taste "goaty." Fresh goat's milk that has been handled properly, however, will be clean-tasting and free from musky or barnyard notes. The milk from many types of goat breeds will produce a rather thin yogurt due to its type of protein and fat content. The milk from Nigerian Dwarf, Nubian, and LaMancha goats typically has more of the right kind of protein, and Nigerian Dwarf and Nubian milk has a higher butterfat content as well, making the milk of either breed a wonderful choice for naturally thick yogurt and kefir. Goat's milk lacks a particular protein (cryoglobulin), present in cow's milk, that causes the fat globules to clump together and rise to the top, giving it a smooth mouthfeel.

SHEEP'S MILK, too, should be clean and pure tasting, but sometimes it is contaminated by lanolin, a waxy substance naturally found in sheep's wool. Lanolin can be present on the animal's udder and accidentally collected during milking, giving the milk and any products made from it an unappealing flavor and tacky mouthfeel. Yogurt and kefir made from high-quality sheep's milk is usually very thick and rich, thanks to its high levels of fat and protein, as well as the type of protein it contains. As with goat's milk, the cream will not separate readily from sheep's milk.

WATER BUFFALO'S MILK makes amazingly rich yogurt. Years ago, I had some made by the former Woodstock Water Buffalo in Vermont. I remember it being the most exquisite yogurt I'd ever had. The richness of water buffalo's milk is unsurpassed. I've heard that yak's milk is similar, but the cream will separate, unlike water buffalo's milk.

Keeping It Fresh

Always remember that aforementioned truism: milk was never meant to see the light of day. Yet the reality of dairy production means that refrigeration and storage are essential. So what do dairy fermenters need to know about their milk and milk source in order to feel comfortable making products for their family and friends?

Store-Bought Milk

Most home dairy fermenters will likely work with store-bought milk. Fortunately, most processed grocery-store milk can be turned into some darned good fermented products. When buying milk at the store, you'll have some information to consider: expiration date (choose the freshest); whether it is ultra-pasteurized, pasteurized, or raw (if you happen to live in a state where it is legal to buy raw milk in a store or from a farmer); fat content (fat-free, 1 percent, 2 percent, or whole); homogenized or cream-top; if it is certified organic; any fortification with vitamins or other nutrients; and whatever marketing terms the company is using to describe its production, such as whether the cows were grass-fed.

We'll cover various heat treatments in chapter 4, but in general, all store-bought milk has been pasteurized. Ultra-pasteurized milk has been heated to a higher temperature, which results in the longest shelf life. Unfortunately this heat treatment also changes the milk proteins and their suitability for making some milk products. While you wouldn't use ultra-pasteurized milk for cheesemaking, you can use it to make yogurt and kefir, and in fact, it will save you a step in the process! (More on that in chapter 8.) Raw milk, where available, has had no heat treatment but often has been produced under some sort of regulatory oversight.

Commercially produced cow's milk is almost always standardized to a set fat content — whole milk to between 3.2 and 3.5 percent butterfat, and skim to between 0.1 and 0.2 percent. Most cow's milk is also put through a mechanical process called

Powdered Skim Milk

Powdered skim milk is commonly used to thicken and increase the protein content in commercially produced yogurts. Skim milk is used for drying since the lack of fat content reduces the chances of rancidity developing. You can use powdered skim milk to make yogurt and kefir, but it's not my first choice, as even the best-quality powdered milks add a cooked, processed flavor that just can't be avoided.

Redwood Hill Farm & Creamery
SEBASTOPOL, CALIFORNIA

I've been lucky enough to know Jennifer Bice, founder and former CEO of Redwood Hill Farm & Creamery, for over a decade. Goats bring a lot of people together, and thanks to magnanimous, kind people like Jennifer, the goat world is a better place. Perhaps even more importantly, the rest of the world is a better place thanks to Redwood Hill Farm & Creamery's pioneering goat milk products.

In 1970, Redwood Hill Farm, founded by Jennifer's parents in the 1960s, debuted the nation's first goat's milk kefir. They chose kefir because its drinkable consistency works well with goat milk and it was a perfect fit for the health-conscious San Francisco Bay Area customers. However, at the time most Americans had barely heard of yogurt, never mind kefir. The product was eventually discontinued, albeit with a small, loyal following. Jennifer remembers loving it as a kid. "It was thick and like a milkshake," she says.

In 1978, Jennifer and her husband, Steven Schack, a fellow goat aficionado, assumed leadership of the struggling farm and dairy. Jennifer was still in college at the time, but the couple wanted to find a way to produce income and keep their goats, so they focused on expanding the milk business.

The revival of the farm was a success. In 1982, they launched the first commercially produced goat's milk yogurt in the United States. By this time, more people were aware of the health benefits of yogurt. In addition, Redwood Hill Farm had an existing solid customer base and distribution network for its milk, which helped jump-start a viable goat's milk yogurt market.

In order to craft a thick product that customers would find appealing and would hold up to transport through the market distribution chain, the couple turned to Jennifer's brother, Kevin Bice. Kevin was pursuing a dairy science degree at Cal Poly and had experimented with many different ingredients for thickening yogurt. He formulated the use of tapioca starch, from cassava root, to create the perfect thickness in the yogurt, without any flavor change or added allergens.

(Tapioca starch is my thickener of choice as well; see how to use tapioca starch in your recipes in the table on page 61.)

For 18 years, Redwood Hill Farm used the services of a co-packer to fill and incubate their yogurt in the cup for them. In 2004, the company built their current spacious, state-of-the-art facility in Sebastapol for producing the yogurt from start to finish. In a smart move, they built it too large. Within a few years, an organic cow dairy they knew and respected lost its milk sales contract. Jennifer knew there was a need for a lactose-free product, so she began buying the cow's milk and quickly put the extra space in their plant to use. In 2010, Green Valley Creamery lactose-free cow's milk yogurt was launched. The brand now also produces lactose-free kefir, sour cream, cream cheese, cottage cheese, and butter. Jennifer says, "We have many lactose-tolerant customers, as the products are so tasty that if one family member needs lactose-free, the rest can enjoy them, too." See the box on page 51 for how to make lactose-free milk at home.

The company has seen much change over their five decades, including the sad loss of Steven, who passed away in 1999. In 2015, Redwood Hill Farm & Creamery, with nation-wide distribution of both brands, passed the reins to the Swiss company Emmi, whose commitment to sustainability and superior management ideals Jennifer liked. She stepped down as CEO after the company's fiftieth anniversary. However, she retains the original Redwood Hill Farm, also known as Capracopia, which is the happy home to not only about 300 dairy goats but also olives, hops, fruit trees, beehives, chickens, and vegetable gardens. Jennifer says that she has come full circle. Not only does she still live at the farm her parents founded, but so does her brother Scott (who is the farm manager) and his wife, Cristi, along with their two children and their own goats.

To learn more about Redwood Hill Farm & Creamery and Green Valley Creamery, including events and tour opportunities as well as goat's milk and lactose-free products, visit their websites (see Resources).

homogenization, which disrupts the fat globules so that they will no longer separate and float to the surface. Only nonhomogenized, cream-top milk is certainly whole milk — that is, it has the natural fat content produced by the animal. (Goat's, sheep's, and water buffalo's milk usually has all of its natural fat content due to its natural state of incorporation.) Unless a recipe specifies a particular fat content, you can use whatever type of milk that you prefer. The higher the fat content, though, the creamier the texture. I'm a believer in full-fat milk, as the vitamins contained in the milk fat globules help our bodies absorb the nutrition in the milk. Thankfully, the medical and science community is again embracing the healthy aspects of full-fat dairy!

Most commercial milk is also fortified with vitamin D, which is added as a way to make up for the vitamin D that is lost when natural fat is removed as part of the standardization process; it also makes up for a typical lack in the average diet. Some milk is also fortified with vitamin A or omega-3 fatty acids — usually in the form of fish oil. Neither vitamin D nor omega-3 fortification will harm milk fermentation. Milk labeled as grass-fed or organic is the most likely to be naturally higher in beta-carotene and have the resulting golden color, compared to the milk from cows fed in total confinement.

Home-Produced Milk

I have so much to say about this topic that I wrote an entire book on it, *The Small-Scale Dairy*, but I'll sum up a few things here. The home milk producer must learn a great deal about animal health and proper milk collection in order to produce safe, delicious milk.

A lot of work goes into the process, but the resulting milk has the potential to be superior to anything you can buy in the store.

Through her milk, an animal can pass diseases (called zoonotic diseases) to humans. In addition, an animal that isn't diseased but isn't vigorous or being fed optimally can harbor extremely dangerous bacteria in her udder — sometimes without any symptoms.

Milk must be collected from healthy animals in an extremely clean fashion, filtered, and then chilled rapidly to prevent the growth of the microbes collected during milking. Factors such as where the animals are milked and how clean the animals are greatly influence the levels of bacteria, yeasts, and molds collected during milking.

If you want to work with raw milk and ferment without doing any heat treatment, then you must understand the importance of good hygiene! If, however, you plan on heat-treating the milk (see page 44), then that step should eliminate any dangers, but remember that the cleaner the milk, the better the flavor.

Farmer-Sourced Milk

You may live in a state where it is possible to purchase milk directly from farmers. Although the sale of Grade A pasteurized milk (the kind you find in every grocery store) is highly regulated by the U.S. Food and Drug Administration (FDA), individual states can have their own regulations allowing for and regulating the sale of unpasteurized milk directly from the farm to the consumer. Typically the regulations set limitations upon the farmers, such as the number of animals they can milk or the volume of milk they can sell. Some states allow what are called herdshares, where the consumer is considered to own all or "part" of a cow, goat, or sheep and pays the farmer to take care of it in exchange for a portion of the milk. The depth and legitimacy of herdshare arrangements vary widely.

If you obtain milk by any of these means, you owe it to yourself and your family to look into the health and safety practices of the farmers. Believe me, any farmers worth buying milk from will embrace your eagerness to learn and will be glad to answer any questions you have. If they aren't transparent with you about their process, then I highly encourage you to seek a different source — even if that is pasteurized milk from the grocery store.

Dairy Milk Deconstructed

Milk is made up of water, fat, proteins, minerals, and a few other minor components. Nature has designed milk to carry these components in the ideal proportions to nourish the appropriate infant. In fact, the composition of a mother's milk changes throughout her

---

Organic and Humane Certified Milk

Organic milk is a good choice if you are looking for certain health benefits as well as some insight into the animal's care. In the health arena, it is well documented that animals that eat naturally (for example, cows grazed on pasture or goats on browse) have a higher percentage of omega-3 fatty acids, which are usually scarce in the typical Western diet. Although nonorganic cows can be fed on grass, you may not be able to tell that from the label on their milk, whereas cows that are managed under organic certification standards must be given a certain amount of time grazing, so you know that milk labeled organic is likely to have higher omega-3 content. Organic standards prohibit the feeding of antimicrobials (aka antibiotics) as a way to boost production. Amazingly, there are antimicrobials (in a group called ionophores) that the FDA has deemed not useful for the treatment of human disease, and so they are therefore considered acceptable as feed supplements for livestock. All milk, whether certified organic or not, must be tested free of several other types of antibiotics to prevent reactions and to prevent the development of antibiotic-resistant microbes. If an animal is ill or injured, whether they are in an organic program or not, the law requires that the animal must be given lifesaving antibiotics, but in order to retain organic certification in the United States, the dairy animal must then be permanently removed from the farm's milk program. (In Europe and Canada, the animal can remain as long as an extended period of time passes in which their milk is not used.)

Humane certification takes organic certification one magnanimous step further in that it addresses all aspects of the animal's care — including treatment of offspring. It allows for the proper treatment of dairy animals with medications, followed by withholding the use of the milk for an extended period of time. This benefits the smaller farmers who aren't likely to be able or even willing to send treated animals away.

---

lactation to meet the changing needs of the growing baby! If you keep that in mind, you'll start to understand why milk from a single source and a small herd can be so variable. When milk is processed on the industrial scale, however, these factors are all but eliminated, due to the milk being collected from any number of farms and a multitude of animals at different stages of lactation, and the subsequent standardization of the amount of fat in the milk. In some respects, this makes working with commercially produced milk easier, as it will be more consistent, even if disappointing to some degree. Let's take a look at the components of milk that are critical for successful fermentation and how those might vary across species, breeds, seasonality, and more.

Water

Milk is mostly water. However, even small variations in the amount of water compared to the solid components — fat, protein, lactose, and minerals — will create different thicknesses of ferments. Sheep and water buffalo are known for their more concentrated (less watery) milk. Within species, different breeds show great variation in the water content of their milk. For example, a big Holstein cow has more diluted milk than a small Jersey cow. Likewise, in goats, the largest dairy breed in the United States, the Saanen, has more water and fewer solids in its milk than the smallest breed, the Nigerian Dwarf. Knowing this information can help you tweak recipes to get the best results possible.

Lactose

This is a complex subject and, quite literally, a complex sugar. Lactose is the conjoined molecule of the sugars glucose and galactose.

You've no doubt heard of glucose, but galactose spends less time in the spotlight, and indeed, it plays a slightly lesser role in milk fermentation. Many adults cannot process lactose — as we learned earlier, their bodies lack the ability to produce lactase, the enzyme that splits lactose into its two simple sugars so that the body can use it. However, the lactic acid bacteria (LAB) that ferment milk also produce the lactase enzyme by which they first split the lactose molecule into glucose and galactose, and then through an extensive pathway of breakdown, produce lactic acid (and in some cases also ethanol alcohol and carbon dioxide gas). The longer the milk ferments, the more lactose the bacteria break down, although there is usually some residual lactose as well as glucose and galactose at the end of the process. For this reason, even people who are moderately lactose intolerant can often digest fermented milk products.

In general, the lactose content of milk decreases toward the end of the animal's lactation, when her baby doesn't need milk as its primary energy source anymore. If you are making yogurt and kefir with milk from your own animals, you might notice that as the animal nears the end of its lactation, the yogurt or kefir takes a bit longer to thicken and get to the desired tartness. This is most often because the LAB have less lactose to consume and so don't produce the same amount of lactic acid as quickly. They may eventually do so, but it just takes longer. (There are other, less likely factors that can also slow fermentation.)

Koumiss is a traditional milk ferment made with mare's milk, which has a much higher lactose content (over 6 percent) than cow's, goat's, or sheep's milk. The additional sugar in mare's milk allows for a greater degree of fermentation, transforming the milk into a beerlike fermented beverage. We'll make a mock koumiss in chapter 6.

Protein

The protein in milk can be divided into two primary categories: caseins (sometimes called cheese proteins, as they are the building blocks of the structure of cheese) and whey proteins (normally lost in the liquid whey during cheesemaking). The total protein content typically ranges from 3 to 4.5 percent, and it is usually a bit lower than the fat percentage of the same milk. On average, cow's milk proteins exist in a ratio of 80 percent caseins to 20 percent whey proteins, while goats have a 70:30 ratio.

There are several types of proteins within the casein group, some of which are the best for making cheese. Cheesemakers add rennet, which causes milk proteins to knit together, or coagulate, forming a gel-like curd, and some casein types are basically better at forming this gel. Yogurt and kefir, however, don't rely upon rennet for their formation. Instead, the acid produced by the fermentation bacteria thickens the milk by causing the milk proteins to stick together rather than repel each other. (An exception is the Icelandic yogurt called skyr, which uses a touch of rennet; see the recipe on page 87.) For this reason, the types of casein proteins in the milk aren't as important to the yogurt and kefir maker as they are to the cheesemaker. However, the total amount of caseins does matter. If you take a look at the chart on page 28, you'll see that the total protein content varies quite a bit between species. The more protein a milk has, the thicker the ferment, and, of course, the resulting product is also a better protein source for us.

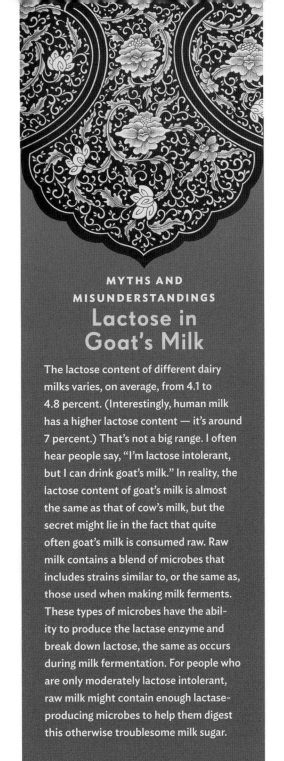

MYTHS AND MISUNDERSTANDINGS
Lactose in Goat's Milk

The lactose content of different dairy milks varies, on average, from 4.1 to 4.8 percent. (Interestingly, human milk has a higher lactose content — it's around 7 percent.) That's not a big range. I often hear people say, "I'm lactose intolerant, but I can drink goat's milk." In reality, the lactose content of goat's milk is almost the same as that of cow's milk, but the secret might lie in the fact that quite often goat's milk is consumed raw. Raw milk contains a blend of microbes that includes strains similar to, or the same as, those used when making milk ferments. These types of microbes have the ability to produce the lactase enzyme and break down lactose, the same as occurs during milk fermentation. For people who are only moderately lactose intolerant, raw milk might contain enough lactase-producing microbes to help them digest this otherwise troublesome milk sugar.

Fat

Milk fat, also called butterfat, varies tremendously by species, breed, stage of lactation, and the animal's diet (interestingly, not from eating fats but from eating the right kind of fiber). Milk fat contributes not only nutritious calories but also pleasing mouthfeel. Fat-soluble vitamins, such as A and D, are contained within the fat globule. The milk fat itself doesn't coagulate but is suspended within the clumped milk proteins. The higher the fat content, in fact, the less firm the curd.

Minerals

Minerals such as calcium don't play the major role in creating yogurt and yogurt-like ferments that they do in the more complex fermenting processes entailed in cheesemaking, where they help rennet coagulate the proteins. But their presence is one of the reasons for the high level of nutrition provided by real dairy ferments. In general, the higher the protein content, particularly the caseins, the higher the mineral content of the milk.

Plant Milks

Plant milks offer alternatives to those with dairy allergies, lactose intolerance, or unanswered concerns about animal welfare. However, plant milks can be challenging to ferment and will create flavor profiles that are quite different than those of their dairy counterparts. If you are trying to create a truly vegan product, you'll have to make sure that the microbial cultures you use are labeled "nondairy" or "dairy-free." I've listed some options in chapter 7; see page 125.

Plant milks don't contain lactose, which is the primary food for yogurt and kefir fermentation bacteria. They also lack milk proteins (caseins), which naturally thicken dairy fermentations. For these reasons, plant milk ferments often include added sugar and thickeners. Remember, the bacteria require sugar in order to ferment, and they will make do with a source that provides glucose (such as table sugar and honey). And added thickener isn't necessarily bad for you. In fact, many thickeners contribute slight nutritional value

Average Milk Components by Dairy Species

ANIMAL	LACTOSE	FAT	TOTAL PROTEIN
Cow	4.8%	3.7%	3.4%
Goat	4.1%	4.5%	2.9%
Sheep	4.8%	7.4%	4.5%
Water buffalo	4.5%	6.0%	4.5%

Sources: P. F. Fox, T. P. Guinee, T. M. Cogan, and P. L. H. McSweeney, *Fundamentals of Cheese Science* (Aspen Publications, Inc., 2000), and R. K. Robinson and R. L. Wilbey, *Cheesemaking Practice* (Kluwer Academic/Plenum Publishers, 1998)

or another health benefit. For instructions on making your own plant milks, see page 120.

SOY MILK is made by soaking dried soybeans and then grinding and straining the mixture to extract the liquid. When made from sprouted soybeans, fresh soy milk can be delicious and quite healthy, as sprouting unlocks some of the otherwise indigestible aspects of fresh soy. Unfortunately, most commercial soy milks are not made from sprouted soybeans. The sugars naturally present in soy milk provide some food for the lactic acid bacteria — usually enough that they can ferment it to close to the same acid level as dairy yogurt. Fresh, homemade soy milk is the best choice, but some fresh, chilled grocery-store versions can work, as long you avoid the shelf-stable variety, which has a lot of additives.

ALMOND MILK is created along the same lines as soy milk. Almonds are soaked and then ground, and the resulting slurry is filtered to remove the liquid. Sugar and thickeners must be added to almond milk in order to convert it to kefir or yogurt. Fresh, homemade almond milk is the best choice, but some fresh, chilled grocery-store versions can work. As with soy milk, avoid the shelf-stable variety.

COCONUT MILK is made from the white flesh of the fruit, which is ground, mixed with hot water, pulverized, and then filtered. Depending on how much water is added, you end up with various versions of coconut milk, from light to cream. Thickeners are needed in varying amounts, depending on the density of the coconut milk, in order to create the familiar thickness of yogurt. Other than fresh, I choose canned coconut milk and cream meant for cooking. It's the least adulterated

Drinkable Almondgurt (page 122)

and the thickest. Coconut milk makes the most flavorful vegan ferment, in my opinion, but I love the flavor of coconut!

There are other plant milks on the market today, including hemp, macadamia, cashew, and rice milks. Most are sold as beverages and include many other ingredients, including thickeners and flavorings. All can be used to make plant milk ferments, but as with other plant milks, you will likely need to add sugar and thickeners.

Microbial Cultures

Microbes — bacteria, yeasts, and molds — are responsible for fermentation. In the case of milk fermentation, it's usually bacteria and sometimes also yeasts. Collectively, these microbes are called culture. As we learned in chapter 1, the microbes that are naturally present in the environment enter the milk at any number of points as and after the milk leaves the animal's udder. (Note: You are unlikely to get a good ferment from wild microbes in plant milks, due to the processing steps of creating the plant milk.) As milk fermenters, we usually have no way of knowing whether these "wild" microbes will help us ferment the milk in a pleasant way or contribute to spoilage — or in the worst case, make someone sick. For that reason, in almost all cases we must add a reliable source of microbes to the milk (although there are still some wild milk ferments happening around the world, and they have some interesting sources for microbes, including even banana leaves). The cultures that we add come powdered (freeze-dried) or fresh (a bit of ferment from a previous batch). Some cultures are heirlooms, having been passed down for generations. We also have what are called kefir grains — clumps of microbial communities used especially for making kefir.

Powdered Cultures

Powdered cultures are produced by a fairly limited number of manufacturers, most of which are located in Europe. These cultures are grown and standardized to ensure that they will produce the right amount of acid, then they are tested for pathogens, freeze-dried, packaged, and given a lot number and expiration date. This makes them the ideal choice for larger producers who must meet

Defining Culture

When used in fermentation and cheesemaking, the word *culture* can be either a noun ("add the culture to the warm milk") or a verb ("it's now time to culture the milk"). The word originated from the Latin *culere*, meaning "to tend" or "to cultivate" (surprise!), and the Latin *cultura*, meaning "growing" or "cultivation." When you add microbes to milk, you are quite literally seeding them into a fertile growth medium. This is the reason that you'll see the words *seed* and *root* also used for living cultures, usually of the heirloom variety.

stringent food safety requirements. They are also quite convenient for home producers, as you can keep them in your freezer and use them as you need. In the resources section as well as near the recipes, you'll find listed just a few of the many suppliers of these powdered cultures.

Powdered cultures are sold in packets (sometimes called sachets) or plastic vials. The culture is freeze-dried, so it will last a long time if stored properly. Keep the packets in the freezer, and do your best to protect them from humidity, as moisture will activate the microbes and then they will perish if not used right away. The best way to keep moisture out is to either use the contents of a packet all at once or reseal and return to the freezer. To protect cultures that come in a vial, open the vial in a dry area (in other words, not right over a steaming pot of milk), and then re-cap and return to the freezer. Also, don't dip your measuring spoon into packets or vials; instead, dispense the powder out of the container into your measuring spoon. This helps prevent moisture and other contaminants from getting in.

Fresh Cultures

You can start all batches of yogurt and cultured kefir with a bit of store-bought product or your previous batch. There's a catch, though — for the best results, the fresh culture source must truly be fresh! As a milk ferment sits, even for a few days, its microbial population diminishes and its microbial variety changes. You might still get decent results using a bit of a less-than-fresh ferment as your culture, but the ferment you make probably won't taste like the batch you took the contribution from. In addition, when you continually reculture from a previous batch, you will likely see a slow but steady decline in the success of that culture (unless it is an heirloom variety). But you won't know unless you try! As long as your ferment thickens and sours in the right amount of time according to the recipe, your concerns won't be about food safety — just aesthetics.

You can also freeze fresh culture. For example, if you make a nice batch of yogurt and want to use some to start your next batch but you don't want to do it soon, freeze it right away. Store it in the coldest spot in your freezer (any partial thawing and then refreezing will damage the hibernating microbes). For instructions on how to freeze cultures, see page 65.

Heirloom Cultures

Heirloom cultures are the sourdoughs of the milk fermentation universe. They are passed down through generations and around to family and friends. In Scandinavia, the dollop of ferment with which a new batch of ferment is started is often called a seed or root. (In the industry, this method is sometimes called slop back, which doesn't sound nearly as appealing!) Heirloom ferments can't be precisely duplicated by freeze-dried cultures, dehydrated cultures, or lab-grown versions. Their exact composition varies depending on many conditions. For all of these reasons, they are known in the industry as undefined cultures.

Unlike modern yogurt cultures, heirloom varieties can regenerate for generation after generation. If you can get your hands on a seed of fresh viili, piimä, filmjölk, matsoni, or one of the other heirloom ferments from the Old World, cherish, nurture, and, above all, share it!

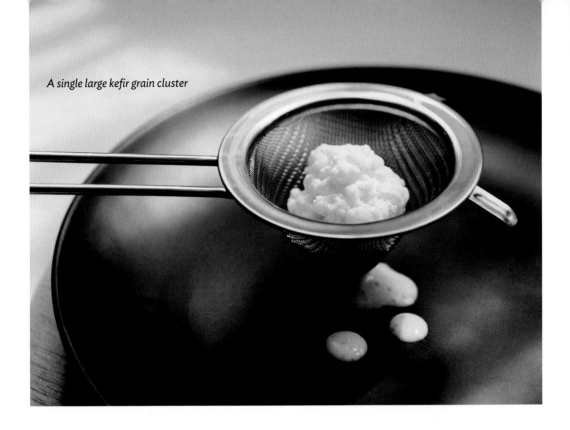

A single large kefir grain cluster

Kefir Grains

Kefir grains are gelatinous clusters created and populated by communities of bacteria, yeasts, and sometimes molds. They are living sources of fermentation microbes. There are two main varieties: milk kefir grains (referred to in this book as simply kefir grains) and water kefir grains. Either can be purchased fresh, dried, or frozen. Milk kefir grains contain microbes that ferment milk sugar, while water kefir grains ferment sucrose (table sugar).

Like sourdough starter, kefir grains must be fed very regularly or their diversity will shift and/or they will die off. Maintaining fresh or reactivated (from dried or frozen) grains is a bit of a commitment — about the level of caring for a goldfish, but with greater rewards. Read more about caring for grains on page 64.

Microbial Diversity

A wide range of wonderful microbes grows well in milk. Some of them are good at converting milk sugar into acid and other by-products, others are good at providing nutrients and support for other milk microbes, and others are best at providing aesthetic nuances and/or probiotics. In milk ferments, they work in collaboration throughout the fermentation. The chart on pages 34 and 35 lists a range of fermentation bacteria and their main contributions to the process. I don't list yeasts here, but when present they all have a similar function: the production of carbon dioxide and flavor.

You'll note in the chart that each bacterial species has a range of temperatures in which it will grow best. When the temperature is below that range, the bacteria won't die, but

A Bit about Taxonomy

The scientific name for any organism is given in Latin, with the genus name first, followed by the species name. The genus name is always capitalized and the species name is always lowercase, such as *Lactobacillus delbrueckii*; in this example, *Lactobacillus* is the genus and *delbrueckii* the species. In quick references to strains, the genus name is often abbreviated: *L. delbrueckii*, for example. In this book, we will deal with two genera (that's the plural of *genus*) with similar names: *Lactobacillus* and *Lactococcus*. To avoid confusion, I'll abbreviate those genus names as *Lb.* (for *Lactobacillus*) and *Lc.* (for *Lactococcus*).

Species are sometimes further divided into subspecies (abbreviated as *ssp.* or *subsp.*); for example, an important fermentation bacteria is *Lactobacillus delbrueckii* ssp. *bulgaricus*. There can also be different strains — for example, *Lb. acidophilus* DSM 20079. Though they may be of the same genus and species, different strains can produce different-tasting fermented products. However, commercial starter cultures don't often list the strains that they use. Furthermore, different companies that use identical strains may give them different names. I know, I know . . . it's complicated. The point is that it's worth sampling several types of starter culture, even those that are labeled with the same bacteria names, and then choosing the one you and your family like the best.

Fermenters also like to divide microbes into two categories related to their ideal growth temperatures. Mesophilic bacteria thrive in moderate temperatures (close to room temperature and a bit warmer). I remember this by thinking about the word *meso,* which means middle (think meso-America). Thermophilic bacteria do best in warmer temperatures, even up to 120°F (49°C). I remember this term by thinking about a thermos — for keeping things hot. (There is a cold-loving category, the psychrophilic microbes, but we won't be covering them in this book.)

---

they will stop reproducing and fermenting. Above that range, they will stagnate or die. *This is why tiny differences in fermentation temperatures can create big differences in the end product.*

Commercial culture manufacturers work hard to create blends of different microbes, including proprietary strains whose designation you likely will never see on the label. Commercial yogurt and kefir makers also work with companies to customize their culture blends to offer something unique to the consumer. At the beginning of the yogurt and kefir recipe chapters, I list some blends I've tried and their sources.

If you are working with an heirloom starter, you are working with a changing population of microbes. Indeed, when an heirloom is passed down, each generation of microbes is likely to change ever so slightly. A healthy heirloom that is well tended should continue to function well, even with population changes over time.

Common Milk Fermentation Bacteria

BACTERIA	GROWTH TEMPERATURE RANGE
Bifidobacterium bifidum, B. breve, B. infantis, B. longum, B. spp.	Mesophile; 72°F–118°F (22°C–48°C); ideal at 97°F (36°C)
Lactobacillus acidophilus	Thermophile; 81°F–118°F (27°C–48°C); ideal at 97°F (36°C)
Lactobacillus casei	Mesophile; 59°F–105°F (15°C–41°C); ideal at 99°F (37°C)
Lactobacillus delbrueckii ssp. bulgaricus	Thermophile; 73°F–125°F (23°C–52°C); ideal at 113°F (45°C)
Lactobacillus delbrueckii ssp. lactis	Thermophile; 65°F–122°F (18°C–50°C); ideal at 104°F (40°C)
Lactobacillus helveticus	Thermophile; 72°F–129°F (22°C–54°C); ideal at 108°F (42°C)
Lactobacillus kefiri	Mesophile; 46°F–109°F (8°C–43°C); ideal at 89°F (32°)
Lactococcus lactis ssp. cremoris	Mesophile; 46°F–104°F (8°C–40°C); ideal at 72°F (22°C)
Lactococcus lactis ssp. lactis	Mesophile; 46°F–104°F (8°C–40°C); ideal at 86°F (30°C)
Lactococcus lactis ssp. lactis biovar. diacetylactis	Mesophile; 46°F–104°F (8°C–40°C); ideal at 72°F–82°F (22°C–28°C)
Lactobacillus plantarum	Mesophile; 59°F–113°F (15°C–45°C); ideal at 99°F (37°C)
Leuconostoc mesenteroides ssp. cremoris and ssp. dextranicum	Mesophile; 39°F–97°F (4°C–36°C); ideal at 72°F–82°F (22°C–28°C)
Streptococcus thermophilus	Thermophile; 73°F–122°F (23°C–50°C); ideal at 113°F (45°C)

PRIMARY FUNCTION	PRIMARY MILK FERMENT APPLICATIONS
Probiotics, acid, and flavor	All
Probiotics and some acid	All
Acid and probiotics	Kefir and kin
Acid and flavor	Yogurt and kin
Acid and flavor	Matsoni and kefir
Acid and flavor	Kefir, koumiss, and other old-world ferments such as matsoni
Acid	Kefir
Acid and texture (some strains produce exopolysaccharides)	Buttermilk, cultured butter, sour cream, kefir, viili, and others
Acid	Buttermilk, cultured butter, sour cream, and kefir
Acid, aroma, and flavor	Buttermilk, cultured butter, sour cream, and kefir
Acid, carbon dioxide, and probiotics	Kefir and kin
Flavor and aroma	Buttermilk, sour cream, and kefir
Acid and texture (some strains produce exopoly-saccharides between 89°F/32°C and 98°F/37°C)	Yogurt and kin

Note: Exopolysaccharides are long chains of natural polymers made up of leftover sugars; they contribute viscosity to the product. See page 59 for details.

chapter 3

Tools and Equipment

Let's start with clearing up the common misconception that you need a yogurt maker to make yogurt. YOU are the yogurt maker (though if you want to buy a basic or a fancy incubator, that's fine, and I'll run through your options). And the tools and processes are so simple that there really are no excuses for not trying to make yogurt, kefir, or any of the other milk ferments included in this book.

Basic Tools

A pot, a spoon, a thermometer, a warm nook: the tools one needs to ferment milk can be exceedingly simple. When choosing your dairy fermentation tools, all you have to do is keep in mind a few simple things in order to make sure that your products turn out as safe and tasty as possible.

Pots and Vessels

Milk can be warmed and fermented in a variety of vessels, but to ensure success, you'll need one that won't react with acid. Unfermented milk is only a tiny bit acidic, but once it begins to ferment acid increases steadily. The acid of the ferment can leach metals from aluminum and even cheap or corroded stainless-steel containers into the ferment. High-quality stainless steel (free from pitting or deep scratches), glass, and crockery are good choices. If you are heating milk to a higher temperature, as in the pre-heating step for making yogurt, you'll want to stick with stainless steel or crockery unless you are sure that the glass vessel is tempered (like a canning jar is), or else it could break during the heating and cooling. Some yogurt incubators include a container made of food-grade plastic, but I personally avoid plastic since the material scratches easily, and some plastics leach unhealthy chemicals into foods when subjected to heat.

Choose a vessel that has a lid so that you can cover it during incubation and with enough room for stirring in the culture without splashing. If you are warming milk in a water bath, then you'll need a second pot or vessel that is able to hold both the warm water and the pot with the milk in it.

Utensils

Spoons, ladles, sieves, colanders, and measuring cups and spoons are some of the most useful implements in dairy fermentation. As with vessels, always choose utensils made of nonreactive materials. Stainless steel, plastic, and wood are all good choices. If you use wooden or plastic spoons, try to dedicate those implements exclusively to dairy

fermentation, as wood and even plastic are great at harboring flavors from cooking. Otherwise your plain yogurt could become a novel flavor such as "beef stew."

Thermometers

In this age of technology, the sky is the limit if you are searching for a fancy way to monitor temperature, including thermometers that will send data to your smartphone! That's not to say, however, that you need anything fancy — I still rely mostly on inexpensive and basic dial thermometers for my dairy fermentation. They have a stainless-steel probe and a dial face, and a small nut on the back allows for calibration adjustments. My next favorite type of thermometer, and definitely more techy, is a wireless grill thermometer. These handy units usually consist of two parts: a heatproof probe and cable attached to a digital unit and a programmable wireless second unit. The heatproof probe and cable mean that you can leave the probe in the pot and not worry about the cable getting hot (for heat-treating milk), and the wireless unit allows you to monitor the temperature of the milk or ferment from a distance.

No matter what type of thermometer you use, **it's important that you calibrate it at regular intervals** to ensure that it is giving you accurate readings. The easiest way to do this is to check the temperature of a glass of ice water to confirm the low range and a glass of boiling water to confirm the high range. In ice water, the thermometer should read just at or above freezing (32°F/0°C), and in boiling water, it should read right around boiling temperature (212°F/100°C). You don't need to factor in your elevation, since fermentation occurs far below boiling temperature and any deviation due to altitude will be almost unnoticeable. I check and adjust my thermometers in ice water alone for that reason.

Draining Tools

When making drained dairy ferments such as Greek-style yogurt or drained kefir, you'll need a few more supplies. You can buy a nifty draining basket specially designed for dairy ferments, with measuring marks so that you can drain the product to the desired moisture content, or you can make your own draining basket simply by placing a piece of fabric over a sieve or colander. If you use the latter method, choose finely woven cheesecloth — about 120 thread count — or polyester organdy (a finely woven, almost sheer, strong fabric) or a woven fabric such as flour sack cloth. You will have to buy real cheesecloth from a cheesemaking or fermentation supplier. The "cheesecloth" sold at grocery and fabric stores is really an open-weave gauze that is designed for straining soup stocks, not yogurt — or even cheese for that matter! A good-quality high-thread-count cheesecloth will last for many years and is worth seeking out.

You must keep cheesecloth and draining baskets very clean. I hand-wash them with dish soap and let them air-dry. Just prior to use, I heat water on the stove to just below boiling, then pour it over the cloth to sanitize it. Allow the cloth to cool to about the temperature of what your dairy ferment is before you pour the ferment into the cloth.

Many references say that you should use a synthetic (such as nylon) or bamboo sieve when you strain kefir grains from a fresh batch of ferment to prevent contact with metals, but in my experience, high-quality stainless steel is fine. As with pots and vessels, you should never use aluminum. Synthetic sieves must usually be ordered; most kitchen supply stores carry only stainless steel.

Incubation Options

To create successful ferments, you need to provide a comfy temperature for the microbes you are trying to cultivate. Some microbes, like those in kefir and many heirloom ferments, do well at room temperature, so all you need to do is set those ferments on the counter and wait. Most others are a bit more finicky and require that you put your ferment in a chamber that will allow you to better control the temperature. Following are some of the many incubation options available in every price range and for every proclivity.

Monitoring pH

As bacteria ferment milk to create yogurt and other products, they make the milk more acidic. If you want to measure how acidic the milk has become, you must measure its pH. The pH scale runs from 0 to 14. The number 7 is neutral. Solutions above 7 are alkaline, and those below 7 are acidic. The pH scale is logarithmic. Simply put, that means that every whole number on the scale marks a pH level that is 10 times greater or lesser than the number above or below it. For example, yogurt that has been fermented to a pH of 5.6 is 10 times more acidic than milk, which has a pH of 6.6. The final pH of yogurt and kefir is closer to 4.3, so that means they are roughly 100 times (10 × 10) more acidic than milk. That's a big difference!

You can use pH strips to test the pH of your ferments, or you can use a handy tool called a pH meter, which will give you a more accurate reading, but they aren't necessary for the home fermenter. If you are a commercial fermenter or are just curious and decide to invest in a meter, you'll need to do a bit of research and, most importantly, read the usage and maintenance instructions that come with your unit. One of the most important aspects of choosing a meter, whether it's a small portable one or a fancier unit — such as my Oakton pH 6 with a glass spear-tip electrode — is to select one whose reading will tell you the pH to the 100ths (for example, 6.55 instead of 6.5). These seemingly tiny differences reflect big differences in acid production.

You can train your taste buds to detect even subtle changes in pH by tasting the ferment at the same time that you check the pH with a meter. Over time, most people can get remarkably adept at this skill.

Use Micro Measuring Spoons

If you are using freeze-dried cultures, a set of micro measuring spoons or scoops is very handy. These little utensils accurately measure very small portions, helping you save money on cultures and keep your batches consistent.

You will find micro measuring spoons labeled with rather archaic terms such as "smidge" and "tad." Although these are fun to say, it's much easier to scale a recipe if you have a more accurate measurement. Here are the equivalents:

Tad = scant ¼ teaspoon

Dash = scant ⅛ teaspoon

Pinch = ¹⁄₁₆ teaspoon

Smidge = ¹⁄₃₂ teaspoon

Drop = ¹⁄₆₀ teaspoon

Ice Chest

The simplest incubation chamber, and my go-to, is a small, well-insulated ice chest. Choose one that easily holds your incubation vessel with a little extra room to tuck jugs of warm water and/or towels around the vessel. I drilled a small hole in the side of mine and stuck a thermometer through the hole so that I can monitor the inside temperature without opening the ice chest. (If you do this, be sure to calibrate your thermometer periodically; see page 38.) I place a towel on the bottom of the ice chest, set the vessel in the middle of the towel, and tuck another towel on top and around the vessel. If the room is cool, I fill one or two jars with warm water (one or two degrees above the ideal incubation temperature) and add them to the chest. When tucked in like this, yogurt will ferment quite evenly.

Warm Oven

A gas oven with a pilot light can be a great option for incubation. Test the oven temperature by setting a thermometer in a glass of water and placing it in the oven, or use a grill thermometer with a heatproof cable. If it exceeds the desired temperature, try opening the door a bit or propping it open with a utensil and see if it will maintain the right temperature. If you don't have a gas oven, you can place a portable light in the oven, which is what my parents did when they first learned to make yogurt in the 1950s. You want the kind of light that comes with a clamp and a screw-on metal cover, and you'll need a traditional incandescent bulb to create the heat (compact fluorescents and LEDs likely won't provide enough heat). For incubating at 110°F to 115°F (43°C to 46°C), use a 100-watt bulb; for incubating at 116°F to 122°F (47°C to 50°C),

use a 200-watt bulb. And be sure to place a sign or other alert on the door noting that the oven is being used for ferments, just in case someone wants to turn the oven on and pop in a batch of cookies while you are fermenting!

Sous Vide

Sous vide means "under vacuum," (because it typically involves heating something in a vacuum-sealed pouch), but the term now also refers to an immersion appliance that both heats and circulates water. The warm water is used as a bath to heat food (or fermentation vessels), and the circulation keeps the water temperature even. Sous vide units are designed to hang on the side of a vessel filled with water and can be adjusted to a wide spectrum of temperatures. They are useful for fermenting. Depending on the size of the vessel and the containers sitting in it, there can be some inconsistency in the water temperature, or even cold spots in certain parts of the container. If you choose this method, be sure to check the temperature of the water bath in various spots until you figure out the quirks of your setup.

Multicooker

I'm a sucker for a good tool, whether for the kitchen or the farm, and the latest and greatest in many people's culinary toolshed is the multicooker. These electric cookers can sear, sauté, simmer, and pressure-cook. Many have a yogurt-making setting that allows you to make batches of yogurt. Some cookers, such as the popular brand Instant Pot, have stainless-steel inserts, while others have nonstick coated inserts. I prefer the stainless steel.

Some milk ferment recipes suggest you heat-treat the milk to denature the proteins and improve the texture of your finished product. Multicookers with a yogurt-making setting often have an option for heat-treating the milk, but I've found it isn't that effective. It's better to heat-treat the milk on your stovetop, cool it, and then use the multicooker for the incubation phase.

You can make your yogurt directly in the multicooker, or you can use it as a hot water bath: fill the insert with water, place the yogurt in glass jars, and place the jars in the cooker with or without a rack. I prefer the water bath approach, so that I don't need to transfer the yogurt to jars once it is done incubating. The water bath also provides a more even temperature.

Unfortunately, there are no precise temperature setting options on multicookers, so if you need to ferment at a temperature that is higher than the default temperature of 110°F/43°C (as in my family yogurt recipe

Going Pro

The growing interest in small-batch, artisan dairy products and probiotics means that making yogurt, kefir, and kin on the small-scale commercial level can be viable. If you are already making cheese or other dairy products, dairy ferments are a great value-added product. Dairy production, however, is one of the most regulated industries in the United States, and undertaking a commercial enterprise requires a lot of research and likely a decent investment of funds.

Regulations vary, but most states follow the FDA's guidelines and regulations regarding yogurt production. These guidelines state that yogurt must be pasteurized and mechanically filled and capped, meaning no ladling by hand or putting lids on the containers by hand. This is quite an impediment to small processors! A couple of states have their own regulations, and as long as the product is only sold within that state, then it is legal. When yogurt is cultured in the cup — without draining, stirring, or mixing — the rules are a bit simpler, but mechanization of some sort is still needed in most cases. Some have talked about creating a loophole for small producers since soft fresh cheeses, which are made in a similar fashion to drained yogurt, can legally be hand-ladled into their containers and capped.

Kefir, skyr, and other dairy ferments aren't subject to the same restrictions, which is beneficial for small producers. You still need a license to produce them on a commercial scale. The word *yogurt* itself is a powerful marketing tool, so it's an unfortunate hurdle for a small producer. There is at least one manufacturer of small dairy equipment (MicroDairy Designs) that has come up with some approaches to meeting this requirement that are acceptable in some states.

For more on small-scale dairy and creamery operations, see the resources section.

on page 74), then the multicooker isn't a good choice.

Electric Yogurt Makers

If you want to purchase a dedicated yogurt maker, there are several options. They vary in price and performance from a simple warming unit to one that will incubate the yogurt and then cool it when it's done. If you are looking at yogurt makers, pay attention to how much yogurt each unit will ferment as well as what type of container holds the milk — plastic or glass. Some units only hold several small cups (6 to 8 ounces each), and others hold a single larger vessel. As I mentioned earlier, I'm not a fan of using plastic to incubate milk, especially at the higher yogurt temperatures. In addition, plastic scratches easily, making it harder to clean and keep sanitary. If you choose a yogurt maker that has glass containers, find out if you can replace them with your own glass jars — such as canning jars — as there's a good chance the original containers will break at some point.

Most yogurt makers are designed to keep the yogurt between 100°F and 110°F (38°C and 43°C) and complete the fermentation in 6 to 8 hours. At least one company has a unit that is set to a lower temperature to ferment over 24 hours. This approach, which is actually referred to as "24-hour yogurt," is meant to give the bacteria enough time to process almost all of the lactose for those who are aren't able to digest milk sugar well or simply want a lower-carbohydrate product.

Bread Proofing Box

Proofers or proofing boxes are appliances designed for raising bread dough. They consist of a lower warming tray, collapsible sides that can stand upright to form a box, and a lid. The temperature can be adjusted (up to 195°F/91°C in slow cooker mode), but in my experience the thermostat is not very accurate. For example, when trying to ferment at 120°F (49°C), I had to adjust the dial up to 185°F (85°C) and then move it up and down to keep the temperature even. This isn't that surprising given that the proofer box isn't insulated — meaning that the ambient room temperature is going to have a tremendous influence on the temperature inside the proofer. So if you want to try one of these otherwise useful units, be sure to place a thermometer inside it and observe the temperature of your milk during fermentation. You can cover the unit with a towel to help keep it warm, and try to put it in a place away from cool drafts.

Food Dehydrator

If you own a food dehydrator with a door and slide-out shelves, then you have a great incubator option. If you own the variety with stacking trays, like I do, you can use it for dehydrating yogurt (page 89) or making yogurt "cookies" (page 215), but jars of yogurt won't fit inside. Food dehydrators have an adjustable thermostat that controls the temperature over the perfect range for making yogurt (and beyond). As with the proofing box, you'll want to verify the temperature by using a thermometer inside the yogurt or a test jar of water, so that you know the yogurt — not just the air inside the dehydrator — is at the right temperature. Dehydrators also include a fan, which isn't needed for incubating yogurt, but it will run nonetheless.

chapter 4

Dairy Fermentation Techniques

Dairy fermentation usually consists of four basic steps: heating, culturing, incubating, and chilling. Other steps might include adding flavors, thickeners, and draining. Once you get the hang of the fer-

mentation process, you can customize your ferment to the tartness, thickness, and flavor you crave. There really is something here for everyone in the family — even those who are lactose intolerant!

Basic Steps for Making Dairy Ferments

At last we get to the nuts and bolts of crafting homemade dairy ferments! The steps outlined in this chapter are relatively simple and easy to master, and they cover the basic techniques for all of the dairy ferment recipes in this book. For a visual step-by-step, see pages 48 and 49.

1. CLEAN YOUR EQUIPMENT

It's a good idea to wash all fermentation equipment both just before and after use. In most cases, it isn't necessary that you sanitize your equipment and tools as long as you have scrubbed and rinsed them with hot water. (If you are a commercial fermenter, though, you should always sanitize your equipment in order to adhere to the "best practices" out-lined in food safety plans.) Woven and mesh draining items are the exception. Because they are absorbent and harder to properly clean, it's a good idea to sanitize them. To sanitize, slowly pour boiling water over the equipment and tools to expose the surfaces to the hot

Sanitizing cheesecloth just before use

water for 30 seconds or use a properly diluted "no-rinse" concentration of chlorine or another food-safe sanitizer (read the label for instructions and use the appropriate test strips to verify sanitizer activity).

Cheesecloths in particular can harbor unwanted bacteria as well as dust and hairs. Hand-wash them immediately after each use and then hang them to dry. If they are bunched up and wet, microbes will start to grow, and the cloths will become smelly, too! If they are dry, microbes cannot grow on them.

When you clean up after fermentation, allow everything to air-dry, rather than using a towel to dry, as this will reduce the possibility of spreading microbes from the towel onto the equipment. A dishwasher works well for washing and drying smaller tools. Reinspect all your equipment and tools before use, and rewash or reclean if needed.

2. HEAT-TREAT THE MILK (MAYBE)

All the ferments in this book require that the milk be at a certain temperature (called the incubation temperature) for optimal fermen-tation. Depending on the recipe, you may first need to heat the milk above the ideal fer-mentation temperature and then cool it back down. This is done to destroy some or almost all of the bacteria in the milk, as well as to denature (change the structure of) some of the milk proteins in order to improve the final texture of your product.

Whether you are working with raw milk or even pasteurized milk, it will contain some bacteria. Raw milk will likely have a lot of microbes, and even though many of them will be harmless or even helpful, they create competition for yogurt and kefir cultures. If you are trying to create a superprobiotic product, then it's often a good idea to give the culturing microbes a blank canvas on which to work. How hot you heat the milk and how long you hold it there will determine how many microbes are killed. Simply put, the hotter or longer the milk is kept hot, the more microbes are destroyed. Note that heating milk on the stovetop will never destroy all microbes. Some types of bacteria, called spore formers, can form protective shells that allow them to survive all but pressure-cooking heat levels. Most of these types of microbes lead to food spoilage over time. This is why an unopened carton of pasteurized milk still "goes bad."

Heating milk to denature its proteins will thicken the final ferment and give it a smoother texture. If you are making kefir or a drinkable dairy ferment, you may not want to denature the proteins because you want a thinner, drinkable consistency. When you make yogurt, however, you generally want to create a thick product. Whey proteins are very heat sensitive. When heated to certain temperatures, they can basically stick to the caseins. This is a bad thing if you are making cheese (as it prevents a good rennet coagulation), but in the case of yogurt, it's terrific! Because they have adhered to the caseins, the whey proteins are retained in the yogurt curd rather than lost in the whey liquid, which increases the yogurt's thickness as well as the total protein content. The degree to which you can thicken the final product depends on the volume of whey protein in the milk (remember, it varies from 20 to 30 percent of the total protein) and on how hot and for how long it's heated. I start by heating the milk to 180°F (82°C) and then experiment with holding it at this temperature for various lengths of time beginning with 10 minutes, or heating it higher, but feel free to play around with temperature and time.

Heat Treatments for Milk

TREATMENT	PARAMETERS	PURPOSE
Thermization	145°F–149°F (63°C–65°C) for 15 seconds	Reduces bacteria count
Low temperature, long time	145°F (63°C) for 30 minutes	Pasteurization
High temperature, short time	161°F (72°C) for 15 seconds	Pasteurization
Scalding to boiling	180°F–220°F (82°C–104°C) for 10–30 minutes	Whey protein denaturing and microbe reduction
Ultrahigh temperature	275°F (135°C) for 1–2 seconds	Pasteurization, whey protein denaturing

3. BRING THE MILK TO INCUBATION TEMPERATURE

The milk must be at the proper incubation temperature, which varies depending on the recipe. If the milk is coming straight from the fridge, you'll have to heat it to the proper temperature. You can use one of several methods: gently heat the milk in a pan directly on the stove or in a double boiler, set the milk container in a bowl of warm water and stir, or pour the cool milk into the incubation jar and warm that in a bowl or pan of warm water.

On the other hand, if you just heated your milk above the ideal incubation temperature in order to destroy bacteria and denature proteins, then you will have to let it cool down before you can add the culture. You can cool your milk very quickly by placing the pot of hot milk in a sink full of cold tap water and stirring the milk to help it cool quickly and prevent a skin from forming on the top. Add more cool water to the sink as needed.

4. ADD THE CULTURE

Marvelous fermentation microbes inhabited the porous utensils and vessels our early dairy producers used, but in modern times, we usually have to add these microbes to our milk to ensure proper and delicious dairy fermentation.

Freeze-dried culture powders come with instructions, and amounts are usually given with quite a range of measurements. Start with the smallest amount recommended and see how the batch proceeds. If it doesn't reach the desired thickness and flavor in the right amount of time, add more culture to the next batch. If it does, you can try adding less the next time. Using accurately measured, small amounts will allow you to conserve your culture and save money over the long run. In general, you should sprinkle the powder on top of the milk, allow it to sit for 1 minute or more, and then stir it in. This allows the fine particles to absorb some moisture so that you can stir them in evenly without having them clump.

If your starter consists of a bit of fresh yogurt or kefir, heirloom seed, or kefir grains, the amount you need will depend upon how fresh the donor batch is — the older it is, the more you are likely to need. It never hurts to add more than you think is required, but it might make the batch ferment more quickly than expected. If you don't mind some inconsistency, then don't worry about it! Generally, you will have good results if you use about 2 tablespoons per quart of milk.

When using fresh yogurt or kefir as the culture, place the amount you need in a small bowl, add a bit of the warmed milk, and whisk together until evenly smooth. Then add the thinned yogurt or kefir to the rest of the milk. Otherwise, the yogurt or kefir is unlikely to stir in evenly and can result in a thick gel only at the bottom of the vessel.

If you're using heirloom seed, you will usually simply mix the seed into the milk directly in the incubation container. The only exception to this is viili, for which you spread the seed over the bottom and sides of the container; see page 111.

If you're using kefir grains, simply place them at the bottom of the container and add the milk, or vice versa.

No matter what type of starter you are using, it's imperative that the milk be at a temperature that will not destroy the fermentation microbes! It's fine if the milk is a couple of degrees above the incubation temperature, as the milk will continue to cool while you are adding the culture.

5. INCUBATE

After you add the culture, it's time to let the milk sit so the fermentation microbes can do their thing. This is called the incubation, ripening, or culturing stage. During this time, even slight temperature variations will affect the texture, acid level, probiotics, and flavor of the finished ferment. Feel free to play around with the temperature range during this stage and see how you like the results. Of course, you can only do this successfully if you are aware of those temperature differences, so plan on having an accurate way to monitor and adjust the temperature. You can also take a more casual approach and simply accept the variations!

Most dairy ferments shouldn't be stirred during the incubation, unless it is early in the process and you aren't confident that the culture has been evenly incorporated or the temperature is even. If you are making a thick product like yogurt, stirring or agitating it in any way toward the gelling stage of incubation might disrupt the formation of the curd. If you are making a drinkable product, don't worry about movement; in fact, gently stirring or rocking kefir or drinkable dairy ferments once or more during their incubation can help create an even texture.

6. CHILL

Once the product has finished its incubation phase, it's important that you cool it as quickly as possible to stop the fermentation. If fermentation continues, the product will become more sour and begin to separate as more whey is expelled from the curd. For the most rapid chilling, cool the product in a cold water bath, set it in the freezer for an hour or two, and then transfer it to the refrigerator. These times are approximate; the smaller the container, the faster your ferment will chill.

There is some wiggle room, especially with warm-temperature ferments like yogurt. You can start the cooling process a bit early by bringing the ferment down to a more moderate temperature; it will continue to develop some acid, but at a slower rate. For example, if a product should ferment for 4 hours and then be rapidly chilled, you could ferment it for 3 hours and then cool in the refrigerator or even for a short period of time on the countertop if that fits your schedule better. Again, as with incubation, you can take a more casual approach as long as you don't mind the variation in the results. Hopefully you are getting the idea that there is a lot of resilience in the entire process!

AT-A-GLANCE HOW TO
MAKE DAIRY FERMENTS

1 **CLEAN TOOLS AND EQUIP-MENT.** Scrub all fermentation tools well, then rinse with hot water and air-dry.

2 **HEAT-TREAT THE MILK** (if needed). Place the milk in a saucepan and heat on the stovetop or in a double boiler over medium heat until it reaches the temperature indicated in the recipe.

3 **BRING THE MILK TO INCUBATION TEMPERATURE** (if necessary). If you heat-treated the milk, fill the sink with cold tap water, then place the pan of milk in the sink and let it cool to the incubation temperature indicated in the recipe. If you need to raise the temperature of the milk, set the milk container in a bowl of warm water and stir.

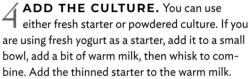

5 **INCUBATE.** Place the cultured milk in an incubator (see page 38 for options) if you are making a warm ferment, or set it on the counter if you are making a room-temperature ferment.

4 **ADD THE CULTURE.** You can use either fresh starter or powdered culture. If you are using fresh yogurt as a starter, add it to a small bowl, add a bit of warm milk, then whisk to combine. Add the thinned starter to the warm milk.

If you are using powdered culture, sprinkle it on top of the warm milk, let sit for 1 minute, and then whisk it in.

6 **CHILL.** Fill the sink with cold tap water or fill a bowl with ice water, and place the incubation vessel in the water until the ferment is cool. Move the ferment to the freezer for 1 or 2 hours, then place it in the refrigerator.

Adding Flavors

Plain yogurt and kefir are great, but, well, plain. Sometimes you just want to play with your food, adding some spice, some sweetness, or some savory notes. Playing with the flavor is also a great way to make the product more versatile so that you can more easily introduce a healthy food to family members who might not yet be adoring fans of dairy ferments. There are no hard-and-fast rules about adding flavors; I'll introduce you to some of my own favorite ideas here, but if you have other ideas, go for it!

Sweetened flavored yogurts have been popular commercially since Dannon debuted them in 1947 in the United States. Savory flavors have appeared on — and disappeared from — the grocery shelves more recently. Two examples are Fage Crossovers (marketed as "chef-level snacking") in combos such as tomato basil with roasted almonds and carrot ginger with pistachios, and New York's famous restaurant empire Blue Hill Farm's carrot, beet, and tomato yogurts. Both sweet- and savory-flavored dairy ferments have long-standing traditions in many cultures. You can even find a cannabis-enhanced version in India (see page 190)! I feel that there will be a continued trend toward and a growing appreciation of these less-sweet flavors.

Sweetness

You can add liquid sweeteners like honey, maple syrup, agave, or simple syrup at any time before or after incubation. Granulated sugars need to be stirred in when the milk or ferment is warm, so that they can dissolve. The amount of sweetener is up to you, but keep in mind that if added before incubation, these sugars will add extra fuel for the bacteria, which can increase the acid level and decrease the final sweetness if they are allowed to continue to ferment. Keep your sweetened finished dairy ferments cold to limit or prevent this.

If you want to make your dairy ferments sweeter but don't want to add any sugar, you can make them with lactose-free milk, which is simply milk to which the enzyme lactase has been added to break down all of the lactose. (In a regular fermentation, there is always some residual lactose remaining at the end of the process.) Once the lactose molecule is split into two simple sugars, glucose and galactose, you can instantly taste the sweetness; your taste buds experience simple sugars as sweeter than more complex sugars. Lactose-free ferments are easy to make. You can use store-bought lactose-free milk with any recipe, or you can create your own lactose-free milk by adding lactase to the ferment at the same time you add the culture (see the box on page 51).

Liquid Extracts and Flavorings

Liquid extracts (natural products) and flavorings (usually not natural) are an easy way to add distinctive taste to your dairy ferment, from the popular vanilla, almond, and lemon to coconut, maple, root beer, and yes, even pumpkin pie spice. Having an assortment and letting your family members flavor their own yogurt or kefir not only is fun for everyone but can encourage consumption. Often adding a bit of extract will give an illusion of sweetness, but without the added sugar.

In most cases, you will add liquid extracts and flavorings to the milk just before you add the culture and incubate it. If you are making a stirred yogurt or drinkable milk ferment,

Homemade, Naturally Sweet Lactose-Free Milk

To make lactose-free milk at home for a sweeter fermented product with no added sugar, just add lactase drops (the easiest choice and available online), the contents of a lactase capsule, or a finely ground lactase tablet to the milk, stir to dissolve, blend, and then refrigerate for 24 to 72 hours. Follow the manufacturer's directions for the quantity of lactase to add and how long to wait (the more lactase you add, the less time it will take for the lactose to break down, but it also depends on how much lactose is in the milk and the temperature). Taste the milk; it should be quite sweet. If a bit of lactose is left in the milk after the lactase treatment, there is a good chance it will be broken down by the lactic acid bacteria during fermentation anyway.

you can add them after incubation. Use ½ to 1 teaspoon of extract or flavoring per quart (4 cups) of milk.

Herbs, Spices, and Citrus Zests

The sky's the limit when it comes to seasoning your dairy ferments. You can add most herbs and spices either before or after incubation. If you add them before incubation, they will yield stronger flavor, but if you add them after incubation, you have more flexibility — a single batch might be divided and flavored in different ways to suit your family members' tastes. Take care with herbs and spices known to have an antimicrobial effect, like sage; they could impede fermentation and should be stirred in after incubation.

When using dried herbs and spices, you'll get the best flavor when you add them early in the process, just before heat treatment or incubation. Fresh herbs are best added after incubation and chilling to maintain their fresh-picked flavor. Here are some herbs and spices that I really enjoy:

CITRUS ZEST. Grated citrus zest adds amazing flavor and a bit of pleasing texture. Add zest just before or after fermentation. If adding after fermentation, the flavor will improve if allowed to sit for a bit of time (overnight in the fridge is usually adequate). Add about 1 tablespoon of grated lemon, lime, orange, or other citrus zest per quart of milk or finished ferment. I don't usually add sweeteners when I use citrus peel, since the peel adds a fruitiness that seems sweet, but you certainly can to make an almost dessertlike treat.

TURMERIC. Turmeric has anti-inflammatory as well as other health benefits, and it gives dairy ferments a beautiful buttery color and nuanced flavor. Add about 2 teaspoons of dried ground turmeric per quart of milk. Incubate as indicated in the recipe. It can go in either a savory or a sweet direction. Try it with a bit of honey, black pepper (the piperine in pepper enhances the health benefits of turmeric), a chai spice infusion, or on its own. I have a premixed blend of turmeric, black pepper (about 1 teaspoon turmeric to ¼ teaspoon black pepper), and a bit of cinnamon, and I mix 1 teaspoon with my fresh glass of kefir. Yummy and healthy!

CINNAMON, NUTMEG, OR ALL-SPICE. These spices lend warm, comforting aromas and flavors to yogurt and other dairy ferments. Add them in a ratio of about ¼ teaspoon of ground spice per quart of milk either before or after incubation.

CURRY POWDER. Curry powder is a mixture of spices that vary depending on the brand. Commonly you'll find it contains ingredients such as turmeric, ginger, cumin, coriander, and pepper. It's great mixed into finished yogurt and even kefir, but use it sparingly; start with ¼ teaspoon per quart of milk. If you are adding it to a drained dairy ferment, you can use a bit more.

Infusions

An infusion is basically a tea, and in dairy ferments, we make a "milk tea" with various herbs and spices to add flavor to our creations. It's most efficient to infuse a portion of the total milk used with the flavoring and then add the infused milk to the rest of the milk. Add the infused milk just before incubation, at about the same time as you add the culture. You can strain the infusion and just add the flavored milk, but if the ingredient you steeped is small and has a pleasant texture (like softened rosemary or lavender), you can add it as well. Here are some infusions I really like; the proportions assume that you will be using the infusion in a ferment of about 1 quart (4 cups) of milk.

COFFEE OR TEA. Heat 1 cup of milk until it just simmers. Turn off the heat and add 1 to 2 tablespoons of ground coffee or tea leaves (any type of tea you enjoy). Stir, cover, and let infuse for 10 minutes. Strain through a fine-mesh strainer or cheesecloth. Coffee and tea infusions are great with chocolate- and amaretto-flavored dairy ferments. If you are a tea lover, you can do what my husband does and simply pour a bit of kefir into your steeped tea!

CARDAMOM PODS, CINNAMON STICK, NUTMEG, OR ALLSPICE. Use these spices in combination or individually to flavor yogurt. Heat 1 cup of milk until it just simmers. Turn off the heat and add 2 teaspoons of slightly crushed whole spices (to crush the spices, use a mortar and pestle or a cocktail muddler, or put them in a ziplock bag and crush them with a rolling pin). Stir, cover, and let infuse for 10 minutes. Strain through a fine-mesh strainer or cheesecloth.

CHAI SPICE BLEND. Heat 1 cup of milk until it just simmers. Turn off the heat and add half of a cinnamon stick, four cloves, and two crushed cardamom pods (you can vary the amounts according to what you like). Stir, cover, and let steep for 10 minutes. Strain and add to the rest of the milk for your ferment. If you like, try adding black tea leaves to the spice mix.

LEMONGRASS. Found in many Thai dishes, lemongrass is a subtle herb that lends itself to both sweet and savory dishes. You can find it in segments or whole, fresh or frozen, in most Asian grocery stores and sometimes even in higher-end natural foods stores. You can also find it dried, but as with many herbs, the dried version is a pale representation of the herb's flavor. To infuse milk with lemongrass, first slice or chop four 1- to 2-inch segments. Bring 1 to 2 cups of milk to a boil, then add the sliced or chopped lemongrass. Turn off the heat, cover, and let stand for 1 hour. Strain and add to the rest of the milk for your ferment.

Herb-Infused Honey

It's easy to infuse honey with herbs, and it makes a wonderful and flavorful sweetener for all kinds of dairy ferments. My favorite herbs for this purpose are lavender and rosemary; they lend beautiful aromatics and flavor when combined with a touch of sweetness.

The proportions are flexible, but I recommend 1 to 2 teaspoons of dried or fresh herb per 4 tablespoons honey. Combine the honey and herb in a small pan (a double boiler is a good choice) and heat for about 10 minutes. Then strain if you don't want to add the herb bits. Add about ⅛ cup warm honey to every quart of milk before incubating, or use the honey to sweeten your ferment as desired once it's done.

Fruit and Veggie Purées

Fruit and veggie purées make wonderful additions to yogurt, adding fiber, flavor, nutrients, and color. As with most flavorings, you are limited only by your imagination — and possibly the produce section at your local grocery store. Purées should be smooth, close to baby food in texture, with minimal chunks so that they don't separate in the yogurt.

Following are some of my favorite fruit and vegetable mixtures. They will flavor 1 to 2 quarts of yogurt or kefir. Put all of the ingredients in a blender or food processor and purée until smooth. Mix with the milk just before adding the culture or after incubation and/or draining. If adding a purée makes your drinkable yogurt too thick, just add milk to thin the mixture.

Mango, Banana, and Lime

This recipe comes courtesy of New England Cheesemaking Supply Company.

½–1 whole mango
½–1 whole ripe banana
2 teaspoons honey
Juice of 1 lime or 1 teaspoon grated lime zest (for thicker results)

Mixed Berries and Roasted Beets

½ cup roasted cubed beets (regular or Chioggia)
½ cup fresh or frozen mixed berries (blueberries, raspberries, blackberries, strawberries, and so on)
1 tablespoon grated orange zest
2 teaspoons honey

Carrot, Ginger, Cinnamon, and Orange

1 cup cubed and cooked carrot or winter squash
1 tablespoon grated orange zest
2 teaspoons honey
½ teaspoon ground cinnamon
¼ teaspoon ground ginger

Indian Shrikhand

This is a classic Indian flavoring mixture usually combined with drained yogurt (*chakka*).

1 cup mashed banana or guava, or combination
2–4 tablespoons honey or another sweetener
¼ teaspoon ground cardamom
Pinch of salt
Tiny pinch of saffron stamens

Chopped Fruit, Jam, and Marmalade

Chunks of fresh fruit, jam, or marmalade can be stirred into any dairy ferment before or after incubation. When added earlier in the process, the fruit chunks tend to settle to the bottom, but this can be a beautiful fruit-at-the-bottom or sundae-style presentation in a glass and fun to eat as well. Use ½ to 1 cup of unsweetened fruit or about ¼ cup of sweet preserves per quart of milk, or to taste.

Sundae-style yogurts with fresh strawberries and blueberries at the bottom

Thickening

Sheep, water buffalo, and other high-fat and high-protein milks usually set into a thick yogurt without any help, but most goat and cow milks will not. If you're looking for a little extra body, mouthfeel, and spoonability, you can either drain your yogurt or add a thickener.

Draining (aka Making Greek Yogurt)

Draining is an age-old technique for creating a thicker, creamier yogurt with less lactose and a longer shelf life. Draining removes most of the residual lactose, which helps prevent further fermentation, keeping the yogurt from growing more tart in the refrigerator. The removal of the lactose also makes the yogurt easier to digest for people who have difficulty digesting milk sugar. Despite the fact that many cultures have been draining their dairy ferments for centuries, drained yogurt is commonly now called Greek yogurt.

To drain yogurt, you'll need to choose one of the draining options, such as cheesecloth and colander or draining basket, mentioned on page 38. Once the yogurt has been incubated, you can drain it immediately or chill it and then drain it later. Simply place the yogurt in the draining basket or cloth-lined colander and cover it to protect it from pets or dust. It should be at a cool room temperature (between 65°F and 72°F / 18°C and 22°C). It helps to stir it every 30 minutes or so during draining. Depending on the thickness desired, the draining time will vary (see the chart on page 58). Once done, stir it well and place in a container, cover tightly, and refrigerate.

What about the Whey?

When you drain yogurt or kefir, you are left with a good portion of the watery liquid called whey. In fact, you can end up with 3 quarts of whey for every gallon of milk you ferment. That's a lot of whey! Commercial Greek yogurt makers face huge challenges dealing with this liquid. Municipal waste management services see whey as a pollutant (due to the amount of oxygen it draws from wastewater as it breaks down), so companies can't just put it down the drain. Fortunately, the home yogurt maker won't have as much whey to deal with, and we can also use it to make other products.

Think of yogurt whey as simply a tangy, drinkable liquid. It contains a bit of lactose, a few minerals, more or less protein (depending on heat treatment), and microbes from the culture. You can use it to flavor and supplement various dishes, such as soups, breads, and even beverages, and feed it to livestock such as chickens and pigs. In part 3 I'll give you recipes for whey mimosas and nonalcoholic punch. If you're not interested in using it for food or feed, you can pour it on a compost pile or around the base of any acid-loving plants, such as berries and conifers.

Dairy Fermentation Techniques

Don't Fear the Ferment

At a recent presentation I was giving, an audience member asked me how I knew it was safe to leave a perishable item like milk sitting out at room temperature for an extended period of time. Here's the short answer: To ensure that the product is harmless, you have to guarantee that enough acid is produced quickly enough to prevent the growth of any unwanted microbes. In the case of raw milk, this means both spoilage and disease-causing microbes; for pasteurized milk, it's simply the spoilage microbes that weren't destroyed by the pasteurization process. As we noted earlier, even if you properly clean and prepare your equipment and tools, spoilage microbes abound in the air and will get into the milk.

The key points to remember for safe milk ferments are:
- Choose high-quality, fresh milk.

- Use well-maintained equipment and clean it well.

- Add starter bacteria from a well-cared-for freeze-dried powder, a measure of fresh ferment, or healthy kefir grains.

- Maintain the proper incubation temperature.

- Verify that the ferment is done by its thickness, tartness, and good aroma and flavor.

Here are a few things that can cause a ferment to fail:
- There's sanitizer residue on the utensils and vessels.

- The incubation temperature is too high or too low.

- The culture is bad (the freeze-dried culture is expired or deactivated, the fresh culture is too old, or the kefir grains have died).

- The milk is contaminated by sanitizer or antibiotics.

- The milk has high levels of contaminating bacteria that outcompete the added fermentation culture.

NOTE: If a ferment doesn't turn out right (for example, it was supposed to thicken in 8 hours but after 12 hours the milk is still thin), then toss it out. Your chickens or your compost pile will thank you.

There's no hard-and-fast rule as to how long you should drain your yogurt or kefir. It depends on how thick your yogurt is to begin with and how thick you want your finished yogurt to be. Milk that has undergone a high-heat treatment to denature whey proteins will produce a thicker yogurt than one made from unheated milk.

Adding Thickeners

Our natural inclination is to suspect "additives" in our food. In fact, health food marketers have so capitalized on this mistrust that additives are now almost an anathema. In truth, a recipe is formed by adding ingredients; in some respects many are additives. Though thickening agents are often categorized as additives, none of the thickeners listed here have any negative health consequences, unless you have an allergy to a particular substance or to its source (for example, if the pectin comes from lemons and you have an allergy to citrus). See the chart on page 61 for how to use each of the following thickeners.

Milk Powder

Adding powdered milk is another tried-and-true way to thicken yogurt, and it is used by many manufacturers. (You might see "skim or low-fat milk" listed as an ingredient if manufacturers start with low-fat milk and dehydrate it themselves as a part of their recipe for making the yogurt.) Using milk powder has the added advantage of boosting the protein and calcium content of the product while lowering the fat content. Milk solids create the creamiest texture of all the thickeners I've tried, but they also change the flavor the most. When using milk powder, choose a high-quality brand for the best flavor.

Gelatin

Natural gelatin is made from animal collagen (the technical name for connective tissue such as cartilage and tendons). Commercial gelatin is most often a by-product from pork and beef processing. In large enough servings, it provides protein and a few other nutrients, but when used to thicken products, the nutritional value is negligible. Gelatin isn't an option for vegetarian, vegan, or kosher (with the exception of pareve gelatin) dairy products.

Gelatin needs to be heated to activate its gelling properties, so if you are making room-temperature ferments, you'll want to heat the milk and gelatin and then cool the mixture back down to room temperature before culturing. Gelatin won't gel until it's

Draining Yogurt

TIME DRAINING (AT ROOM TEMPERATURE OF ABOUT 70°F/21°C)	VOLUME REDUCTION	TEXTURE	COMMON DESCRIPTION
1–2 hours	25%	Slightly thick	Lightly drained
3–4 hours	50%	Medium thick	Moderately drained, Greek, labneh
12–18 hours	75%	Very thick	Fully drained, or yogurt/kefir cheese

Keeping It Together Naturally

Most of us who make yogurt and other dairy ferments don't think too much about what's going on inside the ferment to thicken it, and if you are happy with your end product, then that's just fine. We know that high-fat and high-protein milk will produce a thicker yogurt, but we don't often consider the ability of some microbes in the milk to produce natural stabilizers.

When I was experimenting with the Finnish heirloom room-temperature ferment viili (see the recipe on page 111), I was blown away by the consistency. Quite literally, viili is considered a semisolid. The whey won't separate and it cannot be drained. Why? The answer is in the EPS-producing microbes native to the viili culture. EPS (exopolysaccharides) are long chains of natural polymers made up of leftover sugars. EPS are produced in two forms: one that is long and ropey, and one that is encapsulated. Both increase viscosity by binding water, thereby preventing the watery whey from leaking out of the curd. The longer the chains and the more EPS that are produced, the more viscous the solution. If you've ever worked with xanthan gum — a stabilizer used widely in gluten-free baking, salad dressings, and more — then you've worked with EPS. Once you get a dusting of xanthan gum on your fingers, it takes quite a bit to wash it off because it's so gluey.

Many species and strains of lactic acid bacteria can create EPS given the right conditions. Some strains produce more EPS than others. *Lactococcus lactis* ssp. *cremoris* is well known for its EPS production. Depending on which strain or strains are used (as many as five strains have been isolated from Finnish viili), you can make a product with more or less viscosity. I prefer ABY-2C from GetCulture for yogurt because it creates a slightly viscous result, as does their 901 buttermilk and sour cream culture. I've experienced wild, unplanned gelatinous results when making room-temperature yogurts from raw milk, to the point where the yogurt actually came out of the pot in one gooey glob.

You can play around with strains that produce varying amounts of EPS to nudge your milk ferments in the direction you'd like. If the description of your culture blend includes "thick body" or "suitable for stirred curd (Swiss style)," then EPS producers are likely present. In addition to naturally stabilizing a product, EPS also has probiotic and prebiotic health benefits, so don't worry if your yogurt gets slimed!

cooled, so don't be surprised if your ferment is still runny when you take it out of the incubator. Gelatin won't impact the flavor, but the texture it yields is a bit uneven.

Some common brands of gelatin include Knox (from pork), Great Lakes (from beef), Zint (from grass-fed beef), and NuNaturals (from grass-fed beef). There is even a fish-based gelatin available for kosher and pescatarian diets. I recommend choosing a grass-fed variety, as that helps ensure a healthier product and also a hopefully more natural existence for the animals. I'd love to see a certified humane gelatin one day!

Pectin

Also called fruit pectin, this soluble fiber is usually derived from apples and citrus. It's most commonly used to gel jams and jellies, making it a readily available ingredient in grocery stores. I find that it imparts a smoother texture than gelatin does, unless you use too much. Pectin can be purchased in granular form or as a liquid. Only one brand that I'm aware of has no additional ingredients, and that's Pomona's Pectin.

Most pectin is labeled and marketed with jelly and jam makers in mind, therefore two types of pectin are sold: those designed for low-sugar recipes and those designed for high-sugar ones. In low-sugar preserve recipes, pectin requires a boost from calcium (instead of relying only upon sugars) to perform its gelling magic. Pectins destined for low-sugar recipes contain added calcium, or else a separate packet of powdered calcium is included in the package, which you mix to make to make "calcium water" that is added to the recipe. You don't need extra calcium for gelling dairy ferments, so buy the high-sugar

pectin instead. If you are using the pectin to gel plant-based ferments, you will need to add some calcium, so buy the low-sugar pectin.

Pectin thickens without changing the flavor but creates a bit of an uneven texture. Common brands include Sure-Jell / Certo, Ball, and (my choice) Pomona's Pectin.

Agar

Sometimes marketed as vegan gelatin, agar (or agar-agar) is sourced from a type of seaweed known for its natural gelling properties. The product has some nutritional value, but as with other thickeners, it is usually used in such small amounts that it doesn't contribute much nutrition to milk ferments. Agar sets more firmly than pectin (reminiscent of Jell-O Jigglers), so I recommend it more for use in yogurt and kefir desserts than in the dairy ferments themselves. As with natural gelatin, agar is heat activated. It must be heated to boiling for 5 minutes or to 190°F (88°C) for 10 minutes. It can be heated in water and then added to the ferment if you don't want to heat-treat the milk. Agar thickens without impacting the flavor, but the texture is a bit uneven.

There aren't many brands, but agar powder is usually available at even the smallest natural foods store and can be ordered online.

Guar Gum

Guar gum is made from the seeds of the guar plant from Africa and Asia. It's used as a thickener in many commercial brands of yogurt and lends a smooth, naturally thick consistency. Add a small amount for drinkable products and more for spoonables. It's one of the only thickeners that isn't heat activated, so you can add it when you add the culture or even after the product is done. It's a helpful product for stirred, or Swiss-style, yogurts.

As with agar powder, there aren't many brands, but guar gum is usually available at natural foods stores and online.

Tapioca Starch

Tapioca starch is made from the dried root of the cassava plant (also known as yucca and manioc) native to South and Central America. Tapioca starch is an excellent thickener and is used in many plant-based ferments along with pectin. Occasionally you will see it labeled tapioca flour, but technically tapioca flour is a different product and will not produce the same results. I know — confusing! The starch version is very fine, pure white, and silky to the touch. I really like the smooth and creamy texture of products created by tapioca starch, and it has no detectable taste. It is heat activated but only needs to reach 140°F (60°C) to work.

How to Use Thickeners

TYPE OF THICKENER	HOW MUCH TO USE	HOW TO ADD
Agar	½ teaspoon per quart of milk	Stir into the cold milk, heat to 190°F (88°C) for 10 minutes, and then cool to the incubation temperature. Alternatively, dissolve in ¼ cup cold water and simmer for 5 minutes (the volume will reduce by half), then add to the warm milk just before adding the cultures.
Gelatin	1–3 teaspoons per quart of milk	Stir into the cold milk, heat to at least 120°F (49°C), and then cool to the incubation temperature.
Guar gum	1 teaspoon or less per quart of milk	Stir into the cold milk before heating, or stir into the yogurt after making it.
Milk powder	½–1 cup per quart of milk	Stir into the cold milk before heating.
Pectin	1–2 teaspoons per quart of milk (try the lesser amount first); add an equal amount calcium water when making plant milk ferments	Stir into the cold milk. (For powders, dissolve first in a few tablespoons of cold water and then mix into the cold milk.) Heat, stirring constantly, to 140°F (60°C), then cool to the incubation temperature.
Rennet	Dilute 1 drop of double-strength rennet or 2 drops of single-strength rennet in 4 tablespoons cool, nonchlorinated water; use 1½ teaspoons of this solution per quart of milk	Stir into the cultured milk before incubation. Adjust the amount for future batches according to the desired thickness.
Tapioca starch	2 tablespoons per quart of milk	Stir into the cold milk, heat to 140°F (60°C), and then cool to the incubation temperature. If the milk needs a higher heat treatment, mix the starch with a few tablespoons of cold milk and add at 145°F (63°C), when the milk is cooling down to the incubation temperature.

Bellwether Farms

SONOMA COUNTY, CALIFORNIA

If you've never worked with sheep's milk, it's hard to appreciate how wonderful it is for making all kinds of dairy ferments, from cheese to yogurt. In fact, two of the world's best-known cheeses, French Roquefort and Spanish Romano, are both sheep's milk cheeses. One of the first commercial producers to use ovine milk for yogurt is California's Bellwether Farms, nestled in the rolling green coastal hills of Sonoma County, to the north of San Francisco.

Bellwether (named for the moniker given to the lead sheep, often a castrated male, or wether, who wears a bell to help guide the flock as it grazes) has been making sheep's milk cheeses since 1990. It was founded by Cindy Callahan and is now guided by her son Liam. Cindy and her husband originally purchased the sheep as a way to organically manage the overgrown fields surrounding their 34-acre property. A casual acquaintance of Cindy's planted the idea of milking sheep in her head, and it wasn't long before the dairy was up and running. The cheeses were a hit, and at the time they had no thoughts of expanding into yogurt because low-fat yogurt was all the rage — and if there's one thing sheep don't do well, it's low fat.

By the early 2000s, whole-food products were becoming more appealing and customers were asking the Callahans for a sheep's milk yogurt. In 2005, the company became the second in the nation to sell sheep's milk yogurt (the first being New York's Old Chatham Sheepherding Company). Now, about 75 percent of the milk they process (they also make cow's milk products) goes to making yogurt. All of their sheep's milk comes from East Friesian and Lacaune sheep. In 2018, the company added a line of cow's milk yogurt that Liam says "we always meant to launch, but somehow it took us until then to bring it to the market." Fortunately, their decade-plus of working with their sheep's milk yogurt meant that the transition to cow's milk production was seamless.

Bellwether makes several flavors, including delicious, warming spiced apple. I asked Liam what his favorite flavor is and he replied, "That's a tough question, because I really do love them all. However, I almost always eat the plain — I like to add so much stuff to my yogurt, it's just easier to start out with the plain." His mom's favorite is the strawberry sheep's milk yogurt. "She eats quite a bit of that one," he said fondly. Liam said his kids aren't quite yet keen on either the yogurt or the sheep, but time has a way of winning over even the youngest finicky eaters.

Bellwether has seen many changes over its many years of production. Even though dairy sheep are still quite uncommon in the United States, there are several other producers of sheep's milk yogurt, many of them small crafters selling only locally. Misconceptions about the flavor and properties of sheep's milk are also being set straight. Liam said that in the beginning they were "bombarded with people's fears of 'goatiness' in the yogurt." (Yes, some people think goats and sheep are the same thing.) Now, most people understand and appreciate the unique nature of sheep's milk and seek out its natural richness, digestibility, and deliciousness. If you'd like to sample Bellwether Farms' yogurts, you're in luck — you can find them in many stores across the United States. Visit their website (see Resources) to learn more about their products and find stores near you that sell them.

Rennet

The Icelandic yogurt called skyr is made with rennet, the coagulant used in cheesemaking. In skyr, rennet knits together the milk proteins into a custardlike gel. This is a very effective way to thicken yogurt. I'm actually surprised it isn't used more often! I use vegetarian microbial rennet, but any type will do. (See my recipe for skyr on page 87.)

Rennet comes in two forms — tablet and liquid — and in two strengths — single and double. Liquid rennet must be kept in the refrigerator and protected from light, whereas tablets are shelf stable. Liquid rennet, however, is much easier to measure in small doses. It's important to buy real cheesemaking rennet rather than "junket" rennet, the type often found in grocery stores. Junket rennet will gel but creates bitterness due to its high level of the enzyme pepsin.

Storing Ferments

Store your ferments in sealed containers in the refrigerator. The cold temperature in the fridge will slow but not fully stop the fermentation, so that the ferments will continue to slowly become more acidic as the bacteria process any remaining sugars. This continues until either the bacteria run out of sugar to consume or the product becomes too acidic for even dairy fermentation microbes to survive. The bacteria die off at different rates depending on their acid tolerance and competitiveness; in general, an older ferment will have a lower probiotic count, though it may still taste delicious and be safe to eat. I can't give you an accurate idea of how long the probiotics will remain active, as it completely depends upon the numbers present at the end of fermentation. Obviously, the more you start with, the higher the count will be as time goes by. I try to size batches to last a week, just to be sure.

Remember that spoilage microbes such as mold are present in the air. Every time a container is opened, the surface of the ferment is exposed to these usually unwanted intruders. For this reason, it is better to divide a large batch among several smaller containers and go through them one at a time. If you are too slow to finish a yogurt, kefir, or other milk ferment, you are likely to get some mold growth in the container, particularly along the sides where it's drier. Although most of these molds are unlikely to be harmful, they do ruin the flavor and are a sign that the product is getting old — also your indicator that the probiotics are dying off (an exception is Finnish viili that is traditionally capped with a wrinkly white mold top). You can wipe the edges clean and finish off the product quickly or reseal it in a fresh container. Once opened, yogurt and kefir made from culture should keep their flavor for several weeks. Kefir made from grains will keep its flavor for only a few days, then it gets progressively more sour.

Storing Starter

If you need to take a break from making dairy ferments for more than a few days and don't want to buy new cultures when you get back into the swing of it, you can freeze or dry your fresh starter culture. Both freezing and drying will kill off some microbes, but most microbes will survive if you freeze, dry, and store them correctly.

In my experience, rehydrated kefir grains do a decent job fermenting, but they seem stunted in their growth. Frozen kefir grains will take longer to reactivate and provide adequate acidification.

Freezing

Fortunately, microbes of all kinds survive freezing quite well. They go into a hibernation of sorts, meaning that they don't need any food to survive. When a wet substance is frozen, however, there is risk that it will be damaged by the growth of ice crystals. Yogurt and cultured kefir are very moist, so this risk goes up for them. The best way to control ice crystal growth is to remove as much moisture as possible and then to freeze the cultures rapidly.

FRESH SEED. You can freeze freshly made milk ferments such as yogurt, viili, and even kefir from culture for future culturing. The number of times this will work will depend on the strains of microbes in the ferment. True heirloom ferments, such as viili and Bulgarian yogurt, are likely to do better than something made from powdered cultures, like kefir. It's worth a try, though, if you don't want to be purchasing new starter as often.

Freeze small amounts (about 1 tablespoon). Clean, dry ice cube trays work great! Measure the starter into the trays and place the trays in a supercold freezer; the bottom of a chest freezer works well. When the cubes are frozen, transfer them to ziplock bags (2 to 4 cubes per bag). Seal the bags with a vacuum sealer, or insert a straw partway into each bag, seal the bag around the straw, use your mouth to suck the air out, and then remove the straw and seal the bag fully. Write the date, type of ferment, and volume frozen on the bag and store in the freezer. It should remain viable for about 1 month. Thaw in the refrigerator or by dropping the frozen culture into the milk when it is at the incubation temperature, being sure to rewarm it if the icy starter cools it off too much. Use the same quantity of frozen yogurt culture as fresh.

KEFIR GRAINS. To freeze your grains, drain and rinse them thoroughly with non-chlorinated water. Gently shake them in a strainer for as long as it takes to get all of the moisture off them. When it looks like they are dry, shake the strainer over a dry paper towel to double-check. It's important to remove as much moisture as possible because when the grains are frozen, any moisture will crystallize and damage the structure of the grains. Place the grains in a small bag and, if you want, add a dusting of dry milk powder to absorb any remaining moisture. Remove as much air as possible from the bag, seal, and then freeze in a supercold freezer; the bottom of a chest freezer works well. Frozen grains will remain viable for up to 1 year.

When freezing kefir grains, dust them with a bit of dry milk powder to absorb humidity.

Drying

Yogurt seed and kefir grains must be dried at a very low temperature or the microbes will die. The advantage of drying over freezing is that there's no risk of ice crystals forming and damaging the microbes, meaning that once dried it can remain viable for longer than if frozen. Freezing has the advantage of being quicker and easier, however, making it a great choice for shorter-term storage.

FRESH SEED. Because the volume is reduced by drying and you don't have the risk of ice crystal growth, you can fit twice as much dried yogurt in a single container as you could if you froze it. Place 2-tablespoon portions of culture onto squares of parchment paper and spread to ⅛-inch thickness. Place in a safe spot (away from dust and pests — including your cat) and dry the yogurt slowly at about 80°F (27°C). In low-humidity environments with enough air movement, this might take only a day. Once it is dry, leave the yogurt on the parchment and place in a ziplock bag. Remove as much air as possible, or vacuum-seal it. Write the amount of seed (measured before drying), the type of ferment, and the date it was dried. Store in the refrigerator. When dried properly, it should remain viable for several months. To use dried seed as starter, assume that it has the same volume it had when it was fresh. That is, each square of dried starter will have lost significant volume, but you will treat it as though each portion is 2 tablespoons of yogurt or cultured kefir.

KEFIR GRAINS. To dry grains, rinse them in fresh, nonchlorinated water and drain in a sieve. Break up any very large grains. Lay the grains on a piece of parchment paper and allow to dry for a few days in a warm (about 80°F / 27°C) location safe from pests and dust. Turn them a couple of times by putting your hand under the parchment and moving the grains without touching them. Once they are dry, place them in a ziplock bag. Cultures for Health recommends adding a bit of dry milk powder, which will absorb any humidity. Force all of the air out of the bag, seal, and refrigerate. The dried grains should remain viable for up to 6 months.

Short-Term Storage for Kefir Grains

If you want to take a few weeks off from making kefir, but it's just a short break rather than a months-long sabbatical, you don't need to freeze or dry the grains. Simply drain and rinse the grains, put them in a quart jar, and fill it two-thirds to three-quarters full with milk. Then put the covered jar in the refrigerator. This provides enough food to keep the microbes going, albeit under less than ideal temperatures, so that they slow down significantly. I've heard tales of people keeping their grains in the fridge for a month or longer with no problem, but when I've tried it, I've not liked the changes in the grains — usually they create a ferment that is more yeasty and a bit vinegary. If you're going to stop making kefir for a longer period of time than 3 weeks, I think it's best to dry or freeze the grains.

part two

CORE RECIPES: YOGURT, KEFIR, HEIRLOOM, AND PLANT MILK FERMENTS

chapter 5

Warm Dairy Ferments:
Yogurt and Kin

All of the recipes in this chapter utilize lactic-acid-producing bacteria that prefer warmer temperatures — the thermophiles. Usually these microbes do best between 100°F and 120°F (38°C and 49°C). Depending upon the culture you add and your milk, however, other bacteria that do well at even lower temperatures might also be present. This means that subtle differences in incubation temperature will create subtle differences in the end product. I mention only specific probiotic culture choices, but any yogurt culture will work for every recipe here. In addition, you can scale any recipe up or down to make more or less ferment; just increase or reduce each ingredient proportionately.

Thermophilic Cultures: Some Like It Hot

Micro measuring spoons and powdered, freeze-dried cultures

The transformation of milk into thickened, slightly tart, flavorful yogurt custard requires the work of two very special types of bacteria: *Streptococcus thermophilus* and *Lactobacillus delbrueckii* ssp. *bulgaricus,* which you met in chapter 2. These two types of bacteria are essential for making yogurt. They have evolved a mutually beneficial and reliant relationship during fermentation: In a beautiful partnership, *Lb. bulgaricus* provides metabolites (nutrients for the microbes) that stimulate the growth of *S. thermophilus*, which in turn ferments the milk quickly, producing lactic acid and using up oxygen in the milk, which provides the optimal media for *Lb. bulgaricus*

to then grow. For both to do well, they should be included in the culture blend in approximately equal amounts.

When you're shopping for cultures, you will find that most of them are labeled with the same bacteria names on most of them. But within those groups there will be many different strains, all offering different nuances to the yogurt (see the chart on pages 34 and 35).

Thick, drained Greek yogurt

Probiotic Yogurt Culture Sources

Here are a few of the many options for purchasing probiotic yogurt cultures. I'm a huge fan of the ABY-2C from GetCulture/Dairy Connection for the flavor and texture. I also like that it comes in a little vial instead of packets, making it easier to use small amounts and more affordable in the long run. Most of these companies also have some blends that aren't labeled as probiotic. For a list of heirloom cultures, see page 95.

COMPANY	CULTURE NAME OR CLASSIFICATION	CONTAINS
Cultures for Health*	Mild	*Bifidobacterium lactis, Lactobacillus acidophilus, Lb. delbrueckii ssp. bulgaricus, Lb. delbrueckii ssp. lactis, Streptococcus thermophilus*
GetCulture/Dairy Connection/Cultures for Health	Mild (ABY-2C)	*Streptococcus thermophilus, Lactobacillus delbrueckii ssp. bulgaricus, Lb. delbrueckii ssp. lactis, Lb. acidophilus, Bifidobacterium lactis*
GetCulture/Dairy Connection	Medium (ABY-653)	*Streptococcus thermophilus, Lactobacillus delbrueckii ssp. bulgaricus, Lb. delbrueckii ssp. lactis, Lb. acidophilus, Bifidobacterium lactis*
GetCulture/Dairy Connection/Cultures for Health	Tart (ABY-611)	*Streptococcus thermophilus, Lactobacillus delbrueckii ssp. bulgaricus, Lb. acidophilus, Bifidobacterium lactis*
New England Cheesemaking Supply	Yogurt Starter Sweet (Y5)	*Streptococcus thermophilus, Lactobacillus delbrueckii ssp. bulgaricus, Lb. delbrueckii ssp. lactis, Lb. acidophilus, Bifidobacterium lactis*
Yógourmet	Yogurt Starter	*Streptococcus thermophilus, Lactobacillus delbrueckii ssp. bulgaricus, Lb. acidophilus*

Using Yogurt Seed: Daughter, Root, and Seed Starters

If you use your own yogurt to restart the next batch, called using a daughter, root, or seed starter, its blend of bacteria will continue to change as time goes by, sometimes failing completely after a period of time. (Heirloom cultures, as we'll learn later, have microbes that are better at self-replicating for extended periods, but more modern products utilize microbes that don't self-replicate as well.) This is primarily due to the fact that the different types of bacteria in the culture die off at different rates, with *Streptococcus thermophilus* dying faster than its partner *Lb. bulgaricus*. Since these two critical yogurt microbes need about a 1:1 ratio in order to work properly, the different rate of death negatively changes the reused culture. That being said, you can usually successfully reuse your own yogurt as a starter for some time and simply stop when you no longer like the results! (Chapter 4 gives instructions for freezing and drying dairy ferments for seed.) Here are some options for using yogurt seed (fresh starter):

- **FRESH YOGURT.** Use yogurt that is no older than 1 week. Use at the rate suggested in the recipe.

- **FROZEN YOGURT.** Use yogurt that has been frozen for no more than 4 weeks. Use at the same rate as fresh yogurt, but increase the rate as the yogurt nears the 1-month point of being frozen (and, of course, it never hurts to use more than is recommended).

- **LOW-TEMPERATURE DRIED YOGURT.** Use yogurt that has been dried for no more than about 6 months. Use at the same rate as fresh yogurt (calibrated according to the dried yogurt's original volume when it was fresh, before drying), and break up bits into the warm milk at the culturing step.

Classic Yogurt

This is your core recipe for making almost all yogurts. It is my go-to formula to try with any new type of milk (whether it is a new source or a new species) or any new culture. Once you have made an initial batch, you can evaluate the yogurt's thickness, flavor, and tartness and make adjustments as needed.

Makes ½ gallon

INGREDIENTS

½ gallon milk

⅛ teaspoon powdered yogurt culture or ⅛ cup fresh plain yogurt with active cultures

STEPS

1. Heat the milk to 180°F (82°C) and hold it there for 10 minutes. Then remove the milk from the heat and let cool to 115°F (46°C).

2. Add the culture. If using powdered culture, sprinkle it on top of the milk and let sit for 1 minute, then whisk it in. If using fresh yogurt, combine the yogurt and ¼ cup of the warm milk in a small bowl and whisk until smooth, then add the mixture to the rest of the milk.

3. Incubate at 110°F (43°C) for 8 to 12 hours. Chill and store in the refrigerator.

Gianaclis's Family Recipe

This isn't exactly a "secret" family recipe, but I haven't seen a duplicate of it anywhere in my research. It varies from my classic recipe in that the milk is heated first to boiling and then incubated at the upper limits of the microbes' comfort zone. The result is a very thick yogurt with a milder flavor — and best of all, it's done faster! Since most yogurt incubators and multicookers will only keep the temperature at 110°F (43°C) or so, you'll have to use an alternate incubation method, such as the simple ice chest or food dehydrator. See page 38 for options.

Makes ½ gallon

INGREDIENTS

½ gallon milk

⅛ teaspoon powdered yogurt culture or ⅛ cup fresh plain yogurt with active cultures

STEPS

1. Heat the milk to boiling, stirring frequently and watching carefully to make sure it doesn't boil over. Remove from the heat as soon as it boils and let cool to 125°F (52°C).

2. Add the culture. If using powdered culture, sprinkle it on top of the milk and let sit for 1 minute, then whisk it in. If using fresh yogurt, combine the yogurt and ¼ cup of the warm milk in a small bowl and whisk until smooth, then add the mixture to the rest of the milk.

3. Incubate at 120°F to 122°F (49°C to 50°C) for 4 hours. Chill in a cold water bath for 30 minutes, then chill and store in the refrigerator.

Getting the Most from Goat's Milk

Goat's milk yogurt varies greatly depending on the breed of goat providing the milk. If you are getting milk from one of the breeds that produces milk with high levels of protein and butterfat (such as Nubian or Nigerian Dwarf goats), then you can probably use the Classic Yogurt recipe (page 73) or my family recipe (page 74) and have great results. If your source is one of the many other breeds that makes a lighter milk, then you can do one of the following:

- Increase the heat treatment time and/or temperature.

- Choose a culture with EPS-producing bacteria (see page 59 for more on EPS).

- Drain your yogurt.

- Add thickeners.

I've had great success with goat's milk by using my family recipe and simply increasing the heat treatment temperature and using the culture blend ABY-2C, which has bacteria that improve texture. This is a fast and very effective way to capture as many whey proteins as possible and add viscosity.

Dahi

Dahi (Indian for "curd") is made in a similar manner to classic yogurt, but the higher heat treatment temperature followed by a cooler incubation temperature produces a different final bacteria profile and flavor. I have tried many recipes for this traditional ferment, and I like this one the best. Dahi is the basis for several other milk fermentation products, including chakka (drained curd), mishti doi (sweetened curd, also known as laldahi or payodhi; see the recipe on page 84), and shrikhand (drained curd that's flavored with spices and fruit; see the recipe on page 54).

Makes ½ gallon

INGREDIENTS

½ gallon milk

⅛ teaspoon powdered yogurt culture or ⅛ cup fresh plain yogurt with active cultures

STEPS

1. Heat the milk to 185°F (85°C) and hold it there for 30 minutes. Then remove the milk from the heat and let cool to 100°F (38°C).

2. Add the culture. If using powdered culture, sprinkle it on top of the milk and let sit for 1 minute, then whisk it in. If using fresh yogurt, combine the yogurt and ¼ cup of the warm milk in a small bowl and whisk until smooth, then add the mixture to the rest of the milk.

3. Incubate at 95°F (35°C) for 12 to 16 hours. Chill and store in the refrigerator.

Marketing Mania

Although yogurt has gone by many traditional names over the centuries, in the grocery world, names have as much, or more, to do with attempting to capture a greater piece of the market share than they do with genuine provenance. Here's a list of most of the monikers currently being used on the world yogurt stage. No doubt more are on the way (I'd like to suggest a few myself!).

AUSTRALIAN STYLE: This is a new player on the scene. It is known for being very thick without being drained and often has jam at the bottom.

BULGARIAN: This name claims a relationship to the heirloom yogurts from which the bacterium *Lb. bulgaricus* was isolated; however, all yogurt cultures contain *Lb. bulgaricus*.

CUSTARD STYLE: This is a stirred variety, like Swiss style. Yoplait has been a major user of this term.

FRENCH STYLE: This yogurt is undrained and cultured in the cup; it is sometimes described as "pot set." It likely achieves its thick consistency through the use of reverse osmosis (where water is removed before the yogurt is made). It was premiered by the General Mills Yoplait brand as Oui, which is French for "yes."

FRUIT AT THE BOTTOM: This is another name for sundae style (see next column).

GREEK: Yogurt that has been drained after it is made. The thickness varies depending on the company, as more or less whey can be drained. It is typically drained to be 25 to 50 percent of the original volume of the milk. It is also called labneh.

GREEK STYLE: Usually a yogurt that hasn't been drained but is thick like drained yogurt. The thickness is accomplished by extra thickeners and/or reverse osmosis of the milk.

ICELANDIC STYLE: This is another name for skyr (see below).

LABNEH: See *Greek*.

SKYR: An Icelandic style traditionally made by adding a very small amount of rennet, a coagulant, to thicken the product. Some commercially available brands instead use low-fat milk and then drain it.

SUNDAE STYLE: Yogurt that is cultured in the cup with a bit of sweetened fruit or jam at the bottom. The customer can invert the contents to create an ice cream sundae effect. Also called fruit at the bottom.

SWISS STYLE: A yogurt into which flavorings have been stirred or blended throughout.

Ryazhenka

Ryazhenka, a Russian version of yogurt, is truly distinctive thanks to the overnight baking of the milk, which caramelizes the milk sugars and adds natural sweetness, notes of caramel, and a rich toasted color. The baking also dehydrates the milk, creating a thicker product. When made in the traditional manner, ryazhenka is topped with the golden skin that is created during the baking, producing almost a crème brûlée–like experience.

The milk must not boil but rather cook slowly, to allow time for the sugars and proteins to change and for some of the water to evaporate. You can slow-cook the milk in a variety of ways, including in the oven or a slow cooker. I don't recommend using a multicooker, as it won't caramelize the milk quite as richly, nor will it allow much of a skin to form since the lid cannot be left ajar.

Makes 2–3 quarts

INGREDIENTS

½ gallon milk

⅛ teaspoon powdered yogurt culture or ⅛ cup fresh plain yogurt with active cultures

STEPS

1. If you are using the oven, preheat it to 250°F (120°C).

2. Pour the milk into the crock or pan. If you are using a slow cooker, set it to medium-high. Let the milk heat until it reaches a temperature between 180°F and 200°F (82°C and 93°C). Place the lid slightly ajar on the crock and cook on the low heat setting until the milk is medium brown and a golden to brown mottled skin has formed on top, about 8 hours. Check the temperature of the milk periodically, adjusting the heat setting of the slow cooker as needed to keep the milk in the 180°F to 200°F range (82°C to 93°C).

   If you are using the oven, place the pan in the oven with the door slightly ajar (you can put a metal canning lid ring or a wooden spoon in the door to keep it from closing all the way). Bake the milk for 6 to 8 hours, until it is medium brown and a golden to brown mottled skin has formed on top.

Recipe continues on next page

Ryazhenka *continued*

3. Let the milk cool to 115°F (46°C). If the milk is in a pan that is not glass or crockery, you can do this by setting it in a pan or sink of cool water. Alternatively, you can set your crock or pan on a cooling rack and cover it lightly. Either way, you can encourage cooling by carefully inserting a metal spatula under the skin and moving the milk around gently. If you aren't trying to keep the skin intact, you can stir it in.

4. When the milk reaches 115°F (46°C), peel back a little bit of the skin and scoop out ¼ to ½ cup of the warm milk. Mix the powdered culture or yogurt into this milk, and then stir it into the rest of the milk.

5. Incubate at 110°F (43°C) for 6 to 8 hours. Chill and store in the refrigerator.

Tips for Working with Ryazhenka

If you want to preserve the skin, you will have to be a little careful when mixing in the yogurt culture. I typically blend the skin into the mix. It usually just stays in little pieces and is quite enjoyable that way, not to mention that it's much easier than trying to keep it on top. If you want to create a really stunning presentation, bake and culture the ryazhenka in individual ramekins or custard cups and serve as single servings.

I reached out to an acquaintance in Moscow, Russia, Oleg Boldyrev, a native Moscovite who has been a reporter for the BBC for over two decades, to conduct this interview. Oleg, an avid home cheesemaker, has my book Mastering Artisan Cheesemaking *and has e-mailed me several times over the last few years with cheesemaking questions. I really enjoy my cheesy pen pals and was thrilled when he was willing to help me by seeking out a ryazhenka maker to profile.*

Nina Kozlova

MOSCOW, RUSSIA

Change is often difficult, but sometimes the results are sweet. This is definitely the case for Nina Kozlova, a Russian ryazhenka and yogurt maker. In the early 1990s, the economic upheaval of perestroika (the restructuring of the economic and political system in Russia) left Nina and her husband without jobs. She lost her factory job of assembling television sets in the city of Ryazan, southeast of Moscow, and he lost his job in construction. With work hard to find, the couple moved back to the rural village of Nina's birth.

Nina's mother, who had been making fresh curd, butter, and sour cream for as long as Nina can remember, discovered traditional ryazhenka and decided to make her own at about the same time that Nina returned to the village. Just a few years later, Nina began her own dairy fermentation business. It was a natural fit, Nina says. "We always had cows, and I knew how to make this yogurt — it was always made in front of me."

Every week Nina makes about 50 quarts of individually set containers of traditional Russian ryazhenka. When Oleg interviewed Nina for this profile, he tasted and compared Nina's ryazhenka to a grocery-store brand. He says, "Surely hers is better — richer, with toffeelike notes and clumps of brown from the milk film." Nina also makes plain yogurt, sour cream, butter, and a traditional soft curd cheese called tvorog. The Moscow food cooperative Lavka-Lavka — described by Lonely Planet travel guide as "Moscow's Portlandia" — sells her products in its stores and features her as a vendor at one of its farmers' markets.

Nina works so hard that she doesn't have time to be aware of her part in the growing artisan food movement in Russia. Most dairy producers can relate when she shares, "It's hard — no weekends, no holidays. I can take a week off, but then my daughter or son has to take over — the shops need ryazhenka." Still, her pride shows through when she talks about the care and attention that only a small producer can bring to making this exquisite product, and the opportunity she has for working together as a family. When asked if she would like to expand the

Profile continues on next page

Nina Kozlova *profile continued*

business to meet demand, she replies, "No, I am happy the way it is, otherwise we'd have no time for sleeping. As things are it's me, my daughter, and my son, and my two nieces. That's a family business."

For small-scale artisan food producers, the biggest reward often comes from the reactions of their customers — especially those who know what traditional foods should taste like. Nina says, "Sometimes old babushkas [grandmothers] come in and they say it tastes like their childhood memories. This makes me feel proud."

Sữa Chua
(Vietnamese Yogurt)

France occupied the country of Vietnam from the late 1800s until World War II. During that time, the Vietnamese people assimilated and personalized several Western food traditions, the most well known possibly being the banh mi sandwich, made with a decidedly French baguette. Likely the least well known here in the West is Vietnamese yogurt. The Vietnamese version utilizes canned sweetened condensed milk and some other form of shelf-stable dairy product, such as ultra-pasteurized milk or half-and-half (you can use regular pasteurized milk with just a little difference in texture). This makes sense, as dairy animals and fresh milk are a rare commodity in much of Southeast Asia even today, much less over 100 years ago.

This is not exactly the healthiest version of yogurt that I've included, but it's pretty yummy! The half-and-half and milk add enough flavor balance to mellow out the intense sweetness of the condensed milk. The flavor is subtly caramel. When made in individual bowls or jars, this yogurt makes a wonderful dessert, either plain or with some tart fresh fruit. I wonder when we'll start seeing a widely available commercial version?

Makes about 7 cups

INGREDIENTS

- 1 (14-ounce) can sweetened condensed milk
- 1 cup boiling water
- 3 cups ultra-pasteurized milk
- 1 cup half-and-half
- ⅛ teaspoon powdered yogurt culture or ⅛ cup fresh plain yogurt with active cultures

STEPS

1. Combine the sweetened condensed milk and boiling water in a medium bowl. Stir until the thick milk is thinned and even.

2. Add the milk and half-and-half, and check the temperature. It should be between 110°F and 115°F (43°C and 46°C). If not, warm or cool to that temperature by setting the bowl in another bowl of hot or cold water.

3. Add the culture. If using powdered culture, sprinkle it on top of the milk and let sit for about 2 minutes, then whisk it in. If using fresh yogurt, combine the yogurt and ½ cup of the warm milk in a small bowl and whisk until blended, then add the mixture to the rest of the milk. Pour the mixture into small jars or bowls and cover.

4. Incubate at 110°F to 115°F (43°C to 46°C) for 6 to 8 hours. Eight hours will create a bit more thickness and a bit more tang to balance the sweetness. Chill and store in the refrigerator.

Mishti Doi

This sweetened, condensed traditional Indian yogurt, also called laldahi or payodhi, is a bit of a hybrid between Russian ryazhenka (page 79) and Vietnamese sữa chua (page 82). As with ryazhenka, the milk is baked to condense it and denature the proteins, but it's done at a lower temperature and for a shorter time, so the milk doesn't brown. Then it is sweetened with sugar. For this recipe I used less sugar than many traditional Indian recipes call for and still found it to be plenty sweet!

You'll start with a quart of milk, and by the time it's done baking, it will have lost one-eighth to one-quarter of the original volume — just enough to create a lovely texture. After culturing, you can incubate the yogurt in individual serving sizes and serve it as a dessert topped with a fresh fruit compote, or even with a brûlée crust (see the crème brûlée recipe on page 210).

Makes about 3 cups

INGREDIENTS

- 1 quart milk
- ¼ cup sugar (I prefer raw cane sugar or coconut sugar)
- ¹⁄₁₆ teaspoon powdered yogurt culture or 2 tablespoons fresh plain yogurt with active cultures

STEPS

1. Combine the milk and sugar in a heatproof bowl or baking dish. Turn the oven to the low or warm setting (between 140°F and 160°F/60°C and 71°C).

2. Place the bowl, uncovered, in the oven. Bake for 6 to 7 hours, checking periodically to make sure the milk stays between 140°F and 160°F. (I love my remote grill thermometer for monitoring this.) Then remove the milk from the oven and let cool to 120°F (49°C).

3. Add the culture. If using powdered culture, sprinkle it on top of the milk and let sit for 1 minute, then whisk it in. If using fresh yogurt, combine the yogurt and ¼ cup of the warm milk in a small bowl and whisk until smooth, then add the mixture to the rest of the milk.

4. Incubate at 110°F (43°C) for 8 hours. Chill and store in the refrigerator.

*Coffee-infused
Icelandic skyr*

Icelandic Skyr

This traditional Icelandic yogurt is distinctive in that it uses a touch of rennet to help coagulate the milk. You need only very little; too much will result in a grainy texture. You can use vegetarian or traditional (calf-, kid-, or lamb-sourced) rennet. I recommend using liquid rennet instead of tablets, as it's easier to measure out smaller amounts. Don't use ultra-pasteurized milk in this recipe, as it will negatively affect rennet coagulation.

Some recipes and commercially produced Icelandic yogurts are made using low-fat milk and then drained to create the signature thick consistency. I believe that using rennet is the more traditional method.

Makes ½ gallon

INGREDIENTS

- ½ gallon milk (not ultra-pasteurized)
- ⅛ teaspoon powdered yogurt culture or ⅛ cup fresh plain yogurt with active cultures
- 1 drop (0.05 ml) double- or single-strength rennet diluted just before use in 4 tablespoons cool, nonchlorinated water

STEPS

1. Heat the milk to 180°F (82°C) and hold it there for 10 minutes. Then remove from the heat and let cool to 115°F (46°C).

2. Add the culture. If using powdered culture, sprinkle it on top of the milk and let sit for 1 minute, then whisk it in. If using fresh yogurt, combine the yogurt and ¼ cup of the warm milk in a small bowl and whisk until smooth, then add the mixture to the rest of the milk.

3. Stir in 1 tablespoon of the rennet and water mixture if you are using double-strength rennet, or 2 tablespoons of the mixture if you are using single-strength rennet.

4. Incubate at 110°F (43°C) for 8 to 12 hours. Chill and store in the refrigerator.

Rawgurt

This recipe is for those who want a yogurt-style curd that preserves the enzymes of the raw milk as well as the indigenous microbes. The results will vary quite a bit depending on the type of bacteria in the milk, but that's okay as long as those bacteria are harmless microbes. To ensure the likelihood of this, it's important to watch the incubation time and temperature to give the healthy yogurt bacteria the opportunity to grow rapidly and create an inhospitable environment for any pathogens.

Undrained or otherwise unthickened, rawgurt will be thinner than classic yogurt. Try to work only with superfresh milk. Milk that goes straight from the animal into the incubation vessel is the best — you don't even need to cool it first!

Makes ½ gallon

INGREDIENTS

½ gallon fresh raw milk

⅛ teaspoon powdered yogurt culture or ⅛ cup fresh plain yogurt with active cultures

STEPS

1. Warm the milk to 115°F (46°C).

2. Add the culture. If using powdered culture, sprinkle it on top of the milk and let sit for about 2 minutes, then whisk it in. If using fresh yogurt, combine the yogurt and ½ cup of the warm milk in a small bowl and whisk until blended, then add the mixture to the rest of the milk.

3. Incubate at 110°F to 115°F (43°C to 46°C) for 8 to 12 hours. Chill and store in the refrigerator.

How to Make Dried Yogurt

Virtually every culture with a tradition of making yogurt also has a tradition of drying that yogurt, making products such as *kurat*, *kashk*, and *qurut*. The names and mixtures vary, but the concept is the same — take a staple food and make it portable, durable, and useful. As you might imagine, dried yogurt patties on their own aren't that inspiring to the palate, and indeed, they were not meant to be served as a main course but to be reconstituted in dishes. I initially thought that dried yogurt wouldn't be of much use to modern eaters, but then I thought about camping and backpacking. What a cool thing to be out in the wilderness, pick some wild berries, and mix up a refreshing yogurt parfait! And best of all, the probiotics should still be active as long as the dried yogurt has been stored as described below. On page 215, I'll give you a recipe for yogurt cookies that is an evolution of kurat.

You'll need a dehydrator for this procedure. And note that the lower the fat content of the yogurt, the longer the shelf life of the finished dried product.

1. Partially drain plain yogurt (see tips for draining on page 56).

2. Spread the yogurt as thinly as possible on a piece of parchment or a nonstick dehydrator sheet.

3. Place the yogurt on a tray in a dehydrator and set the temperature to 135°F (57°C). Dry until brittle but not browned, 6 to 7 hours.

4. Break the dried yogurt into bits and place in airtight bags, squeezing out as much air as possible or vacuum-sealing. Use within a week or freeze. If there is any humidity in the bag, the yogurt bits will start to reconstitute; for this reason, vacuum sealing will give you the longest shelf life.

5. When you're ready to use the dried yogurt, mix with water to the desired consistency and enjoy.

Spreading drained yogurt on parchment for drying

Bulgarian Yogurt

This yogurt is made from an heirloom microbial culture. The microbes doing the work are *Lactobacillus bulgaricus* and *Streptococcus thermophilus* — the same as in most yogurts. However, the strains in this particular culture seem to be able to perpetuate themselves through uncountable generations, unlike other yogurt cultures. I'm unsure if this is because the balance starts out differently or because the strains are unique, and I can't find any research providing evidence either way. The resulting yogurt is similar to the other yogurts in this chapter, but it lacks any additional probiotic microbes, or if they are present, they aren't defined. You can get a fresh Bulgarian starter from Savvy Teas and Herbs or a freeze-dried one from Cultures for Health. You may need to make a few batches to get the powdered version back to full activity, and then make a new batch at least once a week to keep the microbes alive and well.

Makes 1 quart

INGREDIENTS

1 quart pasteurized milk

1 packet powdered Bulgarian culture or ⅛–¼ cup Bulgarian yogurt from a recent batch

STEPS

1. Heat the milk to 180°F (82°C) and hold it there for 10 minutes. Then remove from the heat and cool to 115°F (46°C).

2. Add the culture. If using powdered culture, sprinkle it on top of the warm milk and let sit for 1 minute, then whisk it in. If using fresh culture, combine the yogurt with ¼ cup of the warm milk in a small bowl and whisk until smooth, then add the mixture to the rest of the milk.

3. Incubate at 110°F (43°C) for 8 to 12 hours. Chill and store in the refrigerator.

Protein Boost

Many commercial producers add nonfat milk powder to their yogurts to increase the thickness as well as boost the protein content. You can do the same at home. Choose a superior brand of dried milk powder for the best quality. Using skim or low-fat milk, rather than whole milk, will provide even more protein.

Makes ½ gallon

INGREDIENTS

½ gallon skim or partly skimmed milk

¼–½ cup nonfat dry milk powder (look for a high-quality organic brand)

⅛ teaspoon powdered yogurt culture or ⅛ cup fresh plain yogurt with active cultures

STEPS

1. Heat the milk to 180°F (82°C) and hold it there for 10 minutes. Then remove from the heat and let cool to 115°F (46°C).

2. Place about 1 cup of the warm milk in a separate bowl. Slowly add the nonfat milk powder, whisking to break up lumps. Stir the mixture into the rest of the milk.

3. Add the culture. If using powdered culture, sprinkle it on top of the milk and let sit for 1 minute, then whisk it in. If using fresh yogurt, combine the yogurt and ¼ cup of the warm milk in a small bowl and whisk until smooth, then add the mixture to the rest of the milk.

4. Incubate at 110°F (43°C) for 8 hours. Chill and store in the refrigerator.

chapter 6

Room-Temperature Dairy Ferments: Kefir and Kin and Heirloom Yogurts

Countertop ferments are especially easy and appealing — no appliance or special incubation setup required! The bacteria and yeasts that comprise kefir grains and cultures, and those in many heirloom yogurts, prefer moderate room temperatures — anywhere from 65°F to 95°F (18°C to 35°C). In this chapter we'll cover the amazing power of traditional kefir grains, how to use them, and how to care for them. If you don't have the time or inclination to care for kefir grains, which can be demanding, you can also make kefir from powdered culture. I'll cover different options for using powdered kefir cultures, and we'll have some fun with different kefir-inspired recipes.

Kefir Grains: Mysterious Globs of Greatness

Traditional kefir (pronounced both *kee-fur* and *kuh-pheer*) is made possible by the fermentational power of gelatinous microbial globs referred to as milk kefir grains. These knobby masses, often likened to cauliflower florets, are a living system — a symbiotic community of bacteria and yeasts (SCOBY). Kefir grains are an exceptional source of milk fermentation microbes, probiotics, and other healthy compounds. In fact, no other milk ferment quite rivals real kefir for microbial biodiversity (one paper I researched listed over 50 bacterial species and over 14 fungal species in kefir and kefir grains from around the world) and potential health benefits (such as cholesterol reduction, antitumor activity, antimicrobial and antifungal properties, pathogen exclusion in the gut, antiallergenic effects, immune system support, and even faster wound healing through the direct application of kefir grain gels). As I mentioned earlier in the book, we have no record of how kefir grains developed. In addition, no one in modern times has ever reported observing their spontaneous creation. All we know is that they exist, and they vary greatly depending on their care, the milk substrate they feed on, and even where on the planet they live (see the box on page 95).

The kefir SCOBY is rather high maintenance. It needs feeding frequently, ideally about once a week, to maintain a high-quality population of fermentation bacteria and yeasts. When not cared for properly, the ratio of microbes changes, with yeasts and acetobacter bacteria (which make vinegar) often

Kefir grains float when in their maximum fermentation phase.

becoming predominant. This creates a more yeasty, vinegary fermented milk. Research shows that on average, healthy grains consist of 60 to 80 percent lactic acid bacteria, 20 percent acetic acid bacteria, and the rest yeasts. Depending on the proportions of all these microbes, the resulting kefir will vary in flavor and aroma.

Kefir microbes exist inside the gelatinous matrix of the SCOBY, known as kefiran.

Commercial Kefir

It's almost unheard of for commercial producers to make kefir using kefir grains. There are several good reasons for this: it is difficult to retrieve all of the gelatinous grains from the cultured milk; it is hard to predict the fermentation time and acidity; even at refrigeration temperatures, acidity will continue to develop fairly quickly, meaning a short shelf life for flavor; and last, the longer the product sits, the greater the buildup of gases in the carton will be, leading to expanding cartons that will likely explode. For all of these reasons, it is more efficient and profitable to work with powdered kefir cultures.

Kefiran is basically a structure of polysaccharides that won't dissolve in water, so they keep their shape during fermentation. This matrix continues to grow with each feeding, adding housing units, if you will, to provide a place for new microbes to live. Kefir SCOBYs seem to have their own idea of how they should form. Some grains continue to grow in size (see photo on page 32), while others just duplicate themselves as other small grains.

When the kefir microbes reach their exponential growth phase (when fermentation gets serious), they float in the milk. This is one way to observe that they are healthy, active grains. The ideal fermentation temperature for kefir ranges between 68°F and 77°F (20°C and 25°C), and fermentation takes 18 to 24 hours to complete, depending on the volume of grains used. You can modify the temperature and time according to your preferences. Kefir will continue to ferment slowly even at refrigeration temperatures, especially if any fruit or sweetener has been added.

If you want or need to take a break from routine kefir making, there are a couple of options for keeping your grains alive and well; see chapter 4 for details.

Powdered Kefir Culture: The Modern Method

Powdered kefir culture is made from blends of bacteria and yeast that are meant to emulate the fermentation profile of traditional kefir grains. Powdered culture has a couple of advantages over kefir grains: it is more predictable in flavor, usually lacks acetic-acid-producing bacteria, and keeps for a long time between uses. The kefir it makes is mild in flavor and less fizzy, yet distinctive enough from yogurt and from other room-temperature drinkable milk ferments that it stands on its own. In a side-by-side comparison with the fresh buttermilk culture from GetCulture (in which they number 901; it's also great for sour cream and crème fraîche), the difference is quite apparent: the kefir has more bite and just a hint of yeast and bubbles. Although I love buttermilk, I'll choose cultured kefir over it any day thanks to its probiotics and effervescence. If you find that you just don't have the "white thumb" it takes to keep kefir grains healthy and happy, by all means try kefir from culture.

Heirloom Cultures

Heirloom cultures bear the distinction of being able to duplicate themselves indefinitely. This is of great advantage if you don't wish to have to purchase cultures frequently. You can think of kefir grains as worthy of heirloom status, but typically when we say "heirlooms" we are referring to fresh, frozen, or powdered cultures that, once fed, simply have to be fed routinely (like a sourdough starter or kombucha mother) to supply you with another batch of fermented milk. Fresh and frozen heirloom starters are often called a seed or root (as we learned earlier in the book). It is important to follow the instructions that you receive with your first heirloom culture. It is usually recommended that you use pasteurized milk, but really fresh, high-quality raw milk is worth trying — as long as you are prepared to either eventually have it fail or to end up with a distinctive culture thanks to the native flora in the raw milk.

Heirloom Culture Sources and Options

COMPANY	CULTURE NAME OR CLASSIFICATION	FORM
Cultures for Health	Bulgarian, filmjölk, matsoni, piimä, viili	Freeze-dried
GEM Cultures	Filmjölk, viili	Fresh
New England Cheesemaking Supply	Bulgarian	Dried
Savvy Teas and Herbs	Bulgarian, filmjölk, matsoni (they call it Caspian matsoni), viili	Fresh or dried
Yemoos	Filmjölk, viili	Dried

Biodiversity and Geography

Kefer grains have an impressive spectrum of bacteria and yeasts. Scientists studied grains from 13 nations (see "Microbiological Exploration of Different Types of Kefir Grains" in the references) and found that some grains contained no yeasts, while others had four genera, multiple species, and perhaps innumerable strains. Some grains had as many as seven genera of lactic acid bacteria and two species of acetic acid bacteria.

Leading the bacteria diversity list were grains from Belgium and Ireland, with grains from China and Brazil coming in second. When it came to yeasts, grains from Taiwan and Slovenia had the most variety. It's probably safe to assume that even within regions, grains vary widely as well.

It's pretty exciting to think that kefir grains contain that much biodiversity. The grains you get from a friend or a commercial supplier will no doubt develop their own geographical signature given time and exposure to different milks and environment. The bottom line: if you don't love the first kefir grains you try, expand your net and try some others. If you travel, see if you can nab some exotic grains. If you do, let me know!

A healthy batch of small kefir grains

Kefir from Grains

When you receive your first fresh grains, whether from a friend or through the mail, it's important to feed them immediately, even if you aren't ready to make a batch of kefir. If the initial feeding doesn't thicken the milk well within the regular incubation time, strain and rinse the grains and cover them with a new dose of milk. Continue this process until they are vigorous, thickening the milk within the expected time frame. Sometimes it takes a few uses to revive grains. You can still drink the resulting kefir, but expect its flavor to improve and become more complex with successive feedings. Once the grains are quite active (they will float when they are vigorously fermenting the milk), you can store them in their milk in the fridge and ferment with them as infrequently as once a week.

You can use either pasteurized or raw milk, but the kefir grains will grow faster with pasteurized milk. If you use raw milk, use double the amount of grains that's called for in this recipe. The raw milk is also likely to alter the microbial population of the SCOBY, which is just fine, unless you don't like the results.

Makes 1 quart

INGREDIENTS

2–4 tablespoons kefir grains (see note)   1 quart milk

NOTE: *The grain measurement is an estimate. Being globular, the grains are difficult to measure by volume. Since they also vary greatly in how active they are, it's best to simply monitor the results rather than focus on the measurement. In general, the more grains you use, the faster the fermentation.*

Recipe continues on next page

STEPS

1. Place the grains in a jar and cover with the milk (it can be cold or at incubation temperature, but not hot).

2. Place the lid on the jar loosely or just hand tightened (if the yeasts produce a lot of carbon dioxide, you'll want it to be able to escape the jar). Let sit at room temperature, ideally around 70°F (21°C), for 12 to 24 hours. For a slower fermentation, place the jar directly in the refrigerator and let ferment for several days. The flavor will be a bit different with this approach, but if you are having trouble keeping up with consumption, it's a great option! You can gently agitate the jar during fermentation, which will make the final result a bit more even, though this is not necessary.

3. If you're not going to use the kefir right away, chill it in the refrigerator.

4. When you're ready to use the kefir, gently shake or stir the jar. Set a high-quality stainless-steel, synthetic, or bamboo strainer over a glass or jar and strain the kefir through it. Stir the grains in the strainer gently to encourage draining if needed.

5. Rinse the grains with fresh, cool, nonchlorinated water. Place the grains in a clean jar and add more milk to begin the fermentation cycle again.

6. If you don't drink the kefir right away, cover it tightly and refrigerate. It should stay fresh for a few days. It will become more acidic and bubblier as it sits. For an effervescent version, pour the strained kefir into a shatter-proof, stopper-top bottle (such as for beer or kombucha) or a plastic water bottle. Leave 1 or 2 inches of headspace, cap, and store in the fridge for 3 to 4 days. Expect some nice foam when you open it!

Kefir Soda

For a fun fermentation experiment and a delicious, bubbly drink, try doing a secondary fermentation with drained kefir from grains. Add one part fruit juice — such as cranberry, cherry, or apple — to two parts fresh kefir, then bottle in sterilized plastic water bottles or stoppered glass bottles (such as for beer or kombucha). Ferment in the fridge for 1 to 2 weeks. Every few days, gently rock the bottles to blend the ferment. The amount of fizz you get will depend on the sugar content of the fruit juice. If you want a final burst of fizz and a less sour product, add a pinch of baking soda to each glass when serving. Voilà!

Kefir sodas

Kefir from Culture

Even though I have a batch of kefir from grains bubbling away almost constantly, I really enjoy the ease and uniqueness of kefir from culture. It's so reminiscent of cultured buttermilk, but with just a bit more kick thanks to the yeast cultures. If I want to make a kefir cheese, butter, or cream product, it is definitely easier to use powdered culture, since I don't have to strain out the grains. It's also a great introduction to the flavor of kefir, if you or a family member aren't quite ready for the fizzy yeastiness produced by traditional grains. As is the case for yogurt, if you don't want to use a powdered culture, you can start a batch from purchased kefir, since most, if not all, of that variety is made from powdered cultures (see the box on page 94 for why).

Makes 1 quart

INGREDIENTS

1 quart milk

⅛ teaspoon powdered kefir culture or ¼ cup fresh cultured kefir

STEPS

1. Warm the milk to 85°F (29°C). You can gently heat the milk in a pan on the stove and then pour it into the incubation jar, or you can pour the cool milk into the incubation jar and then set the jar in a bowl of warm water to warm.

2. Add the culture. If using powdered culture, sprinkle it on top of the milk and let sit for 1 minute, then whisk it in. If using fresh kefir, combine the kefir with ¼ cup of the warm milk in a small bowl and whisk until smooth, then add the mixture to the rest of the milk.

3. Incubate at 60°F to 75°F (16°C to 24°C) for 12 to 24 hours. Chill and store in the refrigerator.

Powdered Kefir Culture Sources

Different powdered culture blends contain different bacteria and yeasts. Below are a few common brands. You can find contact information for these companies in the resources section, as well as sources of fresh kefir grains.

COMPANY	CULTURE NAME OR CLASSIFICATION	CONTAINS
Body Ecology	Kefir starter	*Lactococcus lactis, Lc. cremoris, Lc. diacetylactis, Leuconostoc cremoris, Lactobacillus plantarum, Lb. casei, Saccharomyces boulardii* (yeast)
GetCulture/Dairy Connection	Kefir Type C	*Lactobacillus casei, Lb. plantarum, Kluyveromyces marxianus* (yeast)
Lifeway	Kefir starter	*Lactococcus lactis, Lc. cremoris, Lc. diacetylactis, Lactobacillus rhamnosus, Kluyveromyces marxianus* (yeast), *Bifidobacterium lactis*
New England Cheesemaking Supply	Kefir starter (C45)	*Lactococcus cremoris, Lactobacillus plantarum, Lc. lactis ssp. lactis, Lc. diacetylactis, Saccharomyces kefir* (yeast)
Yógourmet	Kefir starter	*Lactococcus lactis, Lc. cremoris, Lc. diacetylactis, Lactobacillus acidophilus,* lactic yeasts

Cultured Kefir Buttermilk

Cultured buttermilk is named for its cousin, true buttermilk, which is the liquid remaining after butter is churned (for more on that, see page 133). Cultured buttermilk is slightly tangy and has additional flavors and aromas thanks to the contributions of its bacteria, but it doesn't include any yeasts, so it has a different flavor profile than cultured kefir buttermilk. Bits of butter are sometimes added to commercial buttermilks to create the familiar texture and streaks that coat a glass of the liquid as it empties. We'll accomplish the same by adding a bit of butter to this kefir-based recipe. Ideally, choose a kefir culture that includes the bacterium *Lactococcus lactis* ssp. *lactis* biovar. *diacetylactis*, or *Lc. diacetylactis*, as it's sometimes labeled, for creating a buttery taste and aroma. *Lc. diacetylactis* prefers slightly warmer temperatures (72°F to 82°F/22°C to 28°C) than some of the other kefir microbes. It will still work if you don't provide the extra warmth, but it's fun to experience just how much of a difference temperature makes.

Makes 1 quart

INGREDIENTS

- 1 quart milk
- ⅛ teaspoon kefir culture (ideally one that contains *Lc. diacetylactis*) or ¼ cup fresh cultured kefir
- 1 teaspoon cold butter, finely minced (frozen is the easiest to chop fine)

STEPS

1. Warm the milk to 85°F (29°C). You can gently heat the milk in a pan on the stove and then pour it into the incubation jar, or you can pour the cool milk into the incubation jar and then set the jar in a bowl of warm water to warm.

2. Add the culture. If using powdered culture, sprinkle it on top of the warm milk and let sit for 5 minutes, then stir it in. If using fresh kefir, stir it into the warm milk.

3. Cover and incubate at 85°F to 95°F (29°C to 35°C) for 12 hours, or until thickened. If you are checking the pH, it should be between 4.2 and 4.6.

4. Let the milk cool to room temperature (about 70°F/21°C). Add the butter, cover, and shake to blend the butter throughout and smooth its texture. Chill before serving.

Whey Kefir

If you've made cheese, you know that you end up with a lot of rather extraneous liquid — the whey. Cheesemakers of all scales wrestle with finding disposal options and uses for this by-product. If you happen to have kefir grains and whey, then you are in luck. There is enough residual milk sugar left in the cheese whey to feed the microbes in the kefir grains and convert it into a probiotic, refreshing beverage. Interestingly, research indicates that kefir made with whey — whether it be sweet whey (from making cheeses such as cheddar and Gouda) or deproteinized whey (from making high-heat cheeses with added acid, such as ricotta) — has a similar final microbe profile, and probiotic potential, to kefir made from milk. You can use kefir culture, but I like it best when grains are used.

Whey kefir is great poured over ice with a muddled strawberry and mint leaf.

Makes 2–4 cups

INGREDIENTS

2–4 cups fresh whey from making cheese or draining yogurt

1 tablespoon kefir grains or ¼ teaspoon kefir culture

STEPS

1. Combine the whey and kefir grains or powdered culture in a medium bowl, cover, and let ferment at room temperature for 24 to 48 hours.

2. Strain out the kefir grains, if used, and transfer to another jar. Cover the grains with milk and allow to sit at room temperature for 24 to 48 hours before using again. Enjoy the whey kefir immediately or keep in the fridge. Use within 2 or 3 days.

Koumiss

Traditional koumiss is a slightly boozy, nutritious beverage of fermented mare's milk; it is often fondly referred to as milk champagne. For our recipe, we'll use cow's or goat's milk and shoot for a mild version. By using low-fat milk with added sugar, along with added bacteria and yeast (from kefir or kefir culture), we can come pretty close to the traditional product.

There's quite a bit of wiggle room for experimenting with the ratio of water to milk and sugar. A bit more water will help prevent clumping, but you might need to add more sugar if you increase the water amount. I have played around with using yogurt culture and adding champagne yeast, which worked well and gave the finished product a nice yogurt flavor. Whatever you do, be sure to wrap the bottles in a towel when you agitate them, just in case the pressure exceeds the strength of the glass.

Makes 1 quart

INGREDIENTS

- 1 quart skim milk
- 1 cup water
- 2 teaspoons sugar
- ⅛ teaspoon powdered kefir culture or ⅛ cup fresh kefir

STEPS

1. Pour the milk into a pan and gently heat on the stove to 195°F (91°C), stirring occasionally. Hold it at 195°F (91°C) for 5 minutes.

2. Remove from the heat, add the water and sugar, and let cool to 80°F (27°C).

3. Add the culture. If using powdered culture, sprinkle it on top of the milk and let sit for 1 minute, then whisk it in. If using fresh kefir, combine the kefir with ¼ cup of the warm milk in a small bowl and whisk until smooth, then add the mixture to the rest of the milk.

4. Incubate at warm room temperature (70°F to 80°F/21°C to 27°C) for 6 to 8 hours.

5. Cool to between 65°F and 68°F (18°C and 20°C) by setting the incubation container in a bowl or sink full of cool water and stirring. Hold the temperature between 65°F and 68°F (18°C and 20°C) for 2 hours, stirring every 30 minutes.

Recipe continues on next page

6. Bottle in plastic water bottles or shatterproof, stoppered glass bottles (such as for beer or kombucha) and let cool to 40°F (4°C). Age in the refrigerator for 1 to 3 days, or longer. Before serving, gently agitate the bottles to break up any clumps, then let sit in the fridge for 10 to 20 minutes to let any excess carbonation recede or you may lose a good portion of the contents to foaming when you open it!

Traditional Koumiss

Traditional koumiss is made from mare's milk and is fermented in a horse-skin bag. Koumiss, also called kumiss and coomys, was made by the early Greeks and Romans as well as the horse-centric nomads of Central Asia. It is probably best known, however, as the drink of the Mongolian people, who were introduced to it by a French missionary in the thirteenth century. Taking it one step further, the Mongols even distill koumiss into a hard liquor called arkhi. The alcohol content of traditionally made koumiss is roughly that of a "small beer" — about 3 percent.

Mare's milk is much higher in lactose than the milk of cows, goats, and sheep. It is also lower in fat and protein. Koumiss made from horse milk has a lighter texture (because of the lower fat and protein content) and higher alcohol content (thanks to the extra sugar available for fermentation) than koumiss made from cow's, goat's, or sheep's milk. Although our recipe uses added culture, the original product utilized the raw milk bacteria as well as the bacteria and yeast population that would naturally accumulate in the lining of the horsehide fermentation vessel. Depending on which microbial populations were nurtured in the environment and how long the milk was allowed to ferment, the product varied in acidity and alcohol content.

Filmjölk

This heirloom Swedish fermented milk is quite similar to buttermilk, but I find it to be less tart (even though the pH is the same), and it has a thicker, more luxurious texture. The flavor was very much like that of fresh cream, in fact. I tried two different cultures, one powdered and one seed. The seed culture produced a much better-tasting product. GEM Cultures and Savvy Teas and Herbs both sell seed culture.

Makes 2–4 cups

INGREDIENTS

2–4 cups pasteurized milk

1 packet freeze-dried filmjölk or 2 tablespoons fresh filmjölk

STEPS

1. Combine the milk and culture in a jar and stir well.

2. Cover the jar just loosely, as some gas might form, and let ferment at 65°F to 75°F (18°C to 24°C) for 12 to 24 hours, or until thickened. Then refrigerate.

3. Reculture at least once a week to maintain an active starter.

FERMENTER'S TIP
What about Raw Milk for Heirlooms?

If you have a great source for high-quality raw milk, you are likely to want to use it without messing around with any enzyme-damaging heat treatments. I know that's how I feel when I bring a pail of warm goat's milk up from the barn. However, when working with heirloom cultures, you might want to stick with pasteurized milk, or at least keep a seed culture going on the side using pasteurized milk. Heirlooms can easily be altered by raw milk's natural flora and antimicrobials, leading to loss of fermentation ability or a great change in the resulting flavor. Of course, you also might get lucky and get something even better!

Viili

I LOVE viili! This truly unique Scandinavian heirloom ferment is quite popular in Finland, where it is often eaten for breakfast with cinnamon and sugar. Viili is distinguished by its gelatinous consistency, often described as ropy or slimy. The consistency varies from thin and runny (as in photo) to thick and goopy. The viscosity is thanks to specific lactic acid bacteria that produce high quantities of compounds called exopolysaccharides (EPS; see the box on page 59). Depending on the rate at which the bacteria produce EPS, the product can vary from slightly slimy to an unbroken mass of gel — kind of like the childhood classic "goop."

I tried several viili culture sources and had the best luck with a fresh culture from GEM Cultures in Washington. Powdered and dehydrated versions didn't produce the traditional gloopy characteristic. Viili prefers high-fat milk, so to encourage good batches, periodically ferment a batch using half-and-half or added cream.

Makes 2–4 cups

INGREDIENTS

1–2 tablespoons viili seed

2–4 cups pasteurized milk

STEPS

1. Spread the viili seed across the bottom and sides of a jar or bowl.

2. Pour the milk into the jar but don't stir.

3. Cover the jar just loosely, as some gas might be produced, and let ferment at room temperature for 12 to 24 hours, or until set. Then refrigerate.

4. Reculture at least once a week to maintain an active starter.

Viili's Beneficial Fungus

Heirloom viili has abundant probiotics with proven health benefits. In addition to the probiotic lactic acid bacteria, it often includes the fungus *Geotrichum candidum*, which is more often found on French-style soft ripened cheeses such as Brie and Camembert. This surface-growing fungus produces a mushroomy, earthy aroma and flavor. It grows only on top of the product, however, as it requires oxygen, so the surface area available will affect the degree to which it changes the product. *Geotrichum* is a common environmental fungus, and it likely became a part of traditional viili simply due to its presence in the air. My traditional viili finally grew its own furry top after months of fermenting new batches — it was a delightful surprise to open up the container and find it there! If you want to encourage an earlier growth, you can add a pinch of *Geotrichum* mold culture (available from cheesemaking suppliers) and see how it does.

Piimä

This is a lovely heirloom buttermilk-like ferment originally from
Scandinavia. It's quite thin and tangy. It is a great choice for making
sour cream; just substitute half-and-half or light cream for the milk.
Cultures for Health sells freeze-dried piimä starter.

Makes 2–4 cups

INGREDIENTS

2-4 cups pasteurized milk

1 packet freeze-dried piimä culture
or ¼ cup fresh piimä

STEPS

1. Combine the milk and culture in a jar and stir well.

2. Cover the jar just loosely, as some gas might form, and let ferment at 70°F to
78°F (21°C to 26°C) for 12 to 24 hours, or until thickened. Then refrigerate.

3. Reculture at least once a week to maintain an active starter.

GEM Cultures
LAKEWOOD, WASHINGTON

The go-to online shop for fermentation cultures of many kinds, from kombucha to kefir, sourdough, and miso, is the family-run GEM Cultures in Washington State. The company was founded in Fort Bragg, California, in 1980 by Gordon Edwards McBride (there's the GEM, in case you were wondering) and his wife, Betty. It is now run by Gordon and Betty's daughter and her husband, Lisa and Russ Dunham.

I found GEM when I was searching for an authentic culture for viili — the viscous heirloom ferment originally from Finland. The seed culture I got from GEM is hands-down the most active and gratifying of all of those I tried. There's good reason for that: the fresh culture I used is a direct descendant from the original brought to the United States from Finland over 100 years ago by Gordon's grandparents. It has been lovingly tended by various family members since then and has, quite literally, spread its seed all over the continent.

When I first tried the viili I made from GEM's seed culture, I was quite enamored with its texture and mild flavor. All I could think was how much kids would love to eat and play with it. To confirm my suspicions, I asked Lisa if she had enjoyed it growing up. "We loved viili when we were kids! We ate it the traditional way, with cinnamon and sugar sprinkled on top. The texture is fun — we would try to see how long it would stretch from the spoon to the bowl," she said. She also loved watching her dad spread viili starter inside empty bowls and then add milk before setting the covered bowls on top of the refrigerator overnight to culture for the next morning's portion.

Lisa's Finnish great-grandparents had a large family — 14 children, to be precise! The youngest, Van, expressed at the age of 95 that his greatest concern was that the viili seed he had tended for so long would continue to be cared for. Given GEM's wonderful sharing of fresh viili and the enthusiastic response of milk fermenters everywhere, I think that, somewhere, Lisa's Great-Uncle Van is smiling. To learn more about this gem of a business, visit their website (see Resources).

Matsoni

This heirloom ferment originated in eastern Europe and western Asia, in countries such as Bulgaria, Armenia, Russia, and Georgia. It's also known as matzoon or Caspian Sea yogurt, particularly in Japan, where it can easily be found on grocery store shelves. As far as my research indicates, the predominant bacteria are similar to those found in yogurt (*Streptococcus thermophilus* and *Lactobacillus delbrueckii* ssp. *bulgaricus*), but with the inclusion of myriad other lactic acid bacteria in variations depending on the locality and type of milk. In addition, matsoni contains a variety of yeasts. I had the best results using the fresh Caspian matsoni culture from Savvy Teas and Herbs. It created a delicate gel with a mild tang and pleasant buttery flavor.

Makes 2–4 cups

INGREDIENTS

2–4 cups pasteurized milk

1 packet freeze-dried matsoni culture or ¼ cup fresh matsoni

STEPS

1. Combine the milk and culture in a jar and stir well.

2. Cover the jar just loosely, as some gas might form, and let ferment at 65°F to 75°F (18°C to 24°C) for 12 to 24 hours, or until thickened. Then refrigerate.

3. Reculture at least once a week to maintain an active starter.

Indonesian Dadih

Dadih is a traditional Indonesian ferment made with the rich milk of the water buffalo and fermented in fresh bamboo tubes. Unfortunately, I couldn't find the supplies I needed to duplicate it. In its homeland of Sumatra, the milk is fermented raw, without the addition of any starter bacteria. The milk thickens thanks to the indigenous milk bacteria as well as, it's likely, the natural lactobacilli present in the bamboo and banana leaf, which is used to cover the bamboo tube during fermentation. Water buffalo's milk is much higher in fat and protein than cow's milk and consequently also lower in moisture. As is the case with goat's milk and sheep's milk, the cream doesn't float to the top, so any ferment (such as yogurt or kefir) made with buffalo's milk will naturally be very thick. If you happen to be in Indonesia, or near a water buffalo dairy, a bamboo thicket, and banana tree, give it a try!

chapter 7
Plant Milk Ferments

Whether you are a vegan, have dairy allergies, or just
want to experiment, plant milk ferments are a fun and
tasty alternative to dairy milk. Because they lack lactose
and milk proteins, you need to ferment them differently
than you do dairy milk. Out of respect to the tradition of
dairy as well as the legalities of terminology, I prefer not
to use the terms *yogurt* and *kefir* for these novel ferments.
And, indeed, these plant-based products are unique from
their dairy cousins and deserve to stand on their own. In
most of these recipes, I use dairy-free yogurt cultures.
Several companies offer bacteria blends that are identical
to dairy cultures except that they leave out added ingredients such as lactose or skim milk powder, which otherwise might be used to extend and support the culture.

Soygurt (Vegan)

To make the best soy milk ferment, use pure, plain soy milk that lists only water and soybeans as ingredients, or even better, make fresh soy milk yourself (see page 120). Usually you will find this variety packaged as a shelf-stable product — not in the refrigerator section. If you try to use the fortified, thickened version, you'll end up with a ferment that separates, is clumpy, and has a very chalky mouthfeel. The flavor is also not clean and pleasant like that of real soy milk. Simple soy milk has a lovely balance of fat, protein, and sugar content, similar to that of dairy milk.

You can thicken soy ferments in a variety of ways (see chapter 4 for options). I prefer tapioca starch for the creamier texture it imparts. Once fermentation is finished, some fairly sour and beany notes become apparent, so I like to add a little vanilla extract to balance the final flavor.

Makes 1 quart

INGREDIENTS

- 1 quart plain soy milk
- 2 tablespoons tapioca starch
- ⅛ teaspoon powdered nondairy yogurt culture or ⅛ cup fresh soy milk ferment with active cultures
- ¼–½ teaspoon vanilla extract (optional)

STEPS

1. Combine the soy milk and tapioca starch in a medium saucepan and whisk until well blended.

2. Place the pan over medium heat and warm to 140°F (60°C), stirring constantly. Remove from the heat and let cool to 120°F (49°C).

3. Add the culture. If using powdered culture, sprinkle it on top of the milk and let sit for 1 minute, then whisk it in. If using fresh soy ferment, combine the ferment with ¼ cup of the warm soy milk in a small bowl and whisk until smooth, then add the mixture to the rest of the soy milk. Mix in the vanilla, if using.

4. Incubate at 110°F (43°C) for 6 hours for mild yogurt and up to 8 hours for a more tangy version. Chill before serving. Store in the refrigerator and use within 7 to 10 days.

Coconut Milk
Mock Kefir (Vegan)

When yogurt cultures are incubated at room temperature, the microbes that grow the best create a flavor and aroma profile that is distinct from that of yogurt. Many of these microbes are identical to those you find in kefir cultures, in fact. One key microbe that is missing in yogurt cultures but is present in kefir cultures is yeast. For this recipe I added a bit of *Saccharomyces cerevisiae*, a champagne yeast also often found in real kefir grains. The yeast not only adds complexity and a few bubbles, but it also helps with fermentation. If you want this vegan version of kefir to be more sour, add a teaspoon of table sugar at the beginning. This will provide more food for the bacteria, so they can produce more acid. Coconut milk has a lot of fat, so it can handle a bit more acid and maintain a balanced flavor.

Makes 2 cups

INGREDIENTS

- 2 cups coconut milk
- 1 teaspoon sugar (coconut sugar is a great choice, but any kind will work)
- ¼ teaspoon nondairy yogurt culture with a wide range of microbes, such as any of those from GetCulture or Cultures for Health
- A few grains of champagne yeast

STEPS

1. Pour the coconut milk into a quart jar. Add the sugar and stir until dissolved.

2. Sprinkle the culture and yeast on top and let sit for 3 to 5 minutes, then whisk them in thoroughly.

3. Incubate at 75°F to 85°F (24°C to 29°C) for 24 hours for a mild yogurt and up to 36 hours for a more tangy version. Shake or stir and then chill before serving. Store in the refrigerator and use within 1 week.

Coconut Milk Viili

This recipe is a fun plant milk ferment that's not strictly vegan. I so adore the Finnish milk ferment viili that I thought I'd see what the culture could do to coconut milk. It worked surprisingly well. This doesn't have quite the viscosity of milk viili, but it is very smooth and creamy. The pH dropped to a pleasant tang of 4.2 — the same as that of dairy milk viili. I added a bit of sugar to assist with the fermentation. As with all coconut milk ferments, the pleasant coconut flavor is pleasingly predominant.

Makes 2 cups

INGREDIENTS

1 tablespoon viili seed culture

2 cups coconut milk

1 teaspoon coconut sugar or other sugar

STEPS

1. Spread the viili seed across the bottom and up the sides of a pint jar or small bowl.

2. Combine the coconut milk and sugar in a small bowl, and stir until the sugar is dissolved.

3. Pour the coconut milk into the jar, cover loosely, and incubate at 70°F to 75°F (21°C to 24°C) for 36 to 48 hours. Chill before serving. Store in the refrigerator and use within 1 week.

Make Your Own Plant Milks

Fresh, homemade plant milks really can't be beat for making nondairy ferments. Homemade plant milks have very short shelf lives (only about 3 days) before their quality starts to degrade. Commercially produced plant milks have extended shelf lives, but the processes that increase shelf life don't improve flavor. The exception is canned coconut milk, which is canned very soon after it is made. However, as with other commercially produced plant milks, it usually includes thickeners, stabilizers, flavors, and added sugars that don't make for better-tasting ferments.

Here are some fairly quick and easy steps for making the plant milks we'll work with in this chapter. The instructions below for coconut milk call for dried coconut, but you can also use fresh. You'll need to do some work to remove the coconut meat from the shell, but you can find good instructions online.

Soy Milk

Makes 1 quart

½ cup soybeans

4 cups cold water, plus more for soaking overnight

1. Place the soybeans in a bowl and add enough cool water to cover. Let soak overnight.

2. Drain and rinse the soybeans. Massage them under the water with your hands to remove as many of the firm hulls as possible.

3. Place the soaked and dehulled soybeans in a food processor. Add the 4 cups cold water and process until completely puréed (you will no longer hear the beans or pieces hitting the blades).

4. Line a colander with several layers of cheesecloth, a flour sack cloth, or a nut-milk bag. Set the lined colander inside a large bowl. Pour the soy mixture into the lined colander and let drain. Twist the top of the cloth to squeeze out as much liquid as possible. Use the soy milk immediately, or refrigerate and use within 3 days.

Almond Milk

Makes 1 quart

1 cup raw almonds	4 cups cold water, plus more for soaking overnight

1. Place the almonds in a bowl and add enough cool water to cover. Let soak overnight.

2. Drain and rinse the almonds.

3. Place the soaked almonds in a food processor. Add the 4 cups cold water and process until completely puréed (you will no longer hear the almonds or pieces hitting the blades).

4. Line a colander with several layers of cheesecloth, a flour sack cloth, or a nut-milk bag. Set the lined colander inside a large bowl. Pour the almond mixture into the lined colander and let drain. Twist the top of the cloth to squeeze out as much liquid as possible. Use the almond milk immediately, or refrigerate and use within 3 days.

Coconut Milk

Makes 1 quart

8 ounces dried, unsweetened coconut	4 cups very warm water (120°F–130°F/49°C–54°C)

1. Place the coconut in a food processor.

2. Add the warm water and let sit for about 5 minutes. Then process until completely blended.

3. Line a colander with several layers of cheesecloth, a flour sack cloth, or a nut-milk bag. Set the lined colander inside a large bowl. Pour the coconut mixture into the lined colander and let drain. Twist the top of the cloth to squeeze out as much liquid as possible. Use the coconut milk immediately, or refrigerate and use within 4 days.

Drinkable Almondgurt
(Vegan)

Almond milk has a lovely, lightly sweet, and only slightly nutty flavor. Yogurt made from almond milk has a similar flavor, but with a pleasant tartness and mild yogurtlike flavor. Fresh almond milk makes the best ferment, though plain, unsweetened, refrigerated (not shelf-stable) almond milk from the grocery store ferments just fine in my experience. (I've read many blogs that claim the contrary, but I haven't had a problem fermenting store-bought almond milk.) If you'd like a tarter version, you can add about 1 teaspoon of sugar per 2 cups of milk (mine got to a pH of 4.38 without sugar and 4.27 with). I like to add a bit of guar gum to improve mouthfeel, but it's completely optional.

To keep this recipe super easy, we're going to ferment it right in the carton and incubate in an ice chest. Of course, you can do it in a jar if you prefer!

Makes 1 quart

INGREDIENTS

1 quart plain, unsweetened almond milk

2 teaspoons raw sugar or honey

¼ teaspoon powdered nondairy yogurt culture

1 teaspoon guar gum (optional)

STEPS

1. Pour 1 cup of the almond milk into a bowl. Add the sugar, culture, and guar gum, if using, and whisk until the solids are dissolved.

2. Warm the remaining 3 cups of almond milk in a small saucepan to 120°F (49°C), stirring constantly, and then remove from the heat. Pour the almond milk and sugar mixture into the warm milk and stir to dissolve.

3. Pour the milk back into the carton, close loosely, and place in an ice chest. Incubate for 8 to 10 hours, or until you reach the desired level of tartness. You don't need to rewarm the mixture. Shake gently, then chill before serving. Store in the refrigerator and use within 7 to 10 days.

Springfield Creamery and Nancy's Yogurt

EUGENE, OREGON

Sometimes the stars align and a beautiful constellation appears. In the case of Nancy's Yogurt and Springfield Creamery, it might be telling that stars both literal (adorning their packaging) and figurative (aka the Grateful Dead and Huey Lewis) feature in the company's story. Founded as Springfield Creamery in 1960 in Springfield, Oregon, by Chuck Kesey and Sue Kesey (wait, there is a Nancy in the story), Nancy's Yogurt is a pioneer in the world of dairy ferments. And it's a success story; their products have been sold in all 50 states and in Canada since the mid-1990s and the company is a source of pride for Oregonians.

The business began by bottling and distributing milk to homes and schools in the Springfield-Eugene area. Before the 1960s were over, Chuck and Sue were looking for a value-added product — a way to increase their revenue stream using their readily available supply of quality local milk. The timing coincided with the growing interest in natural, whole, real food. Chuck, who has a degree in dairy science, was aware of the growing interest in using the probiotic bacteria *Lactobacillus acidophilus* in dairy products. Then Nancy arrived.

A yogurt afficianado from the San Francisco Bay Area, Nancy V. Brasch Hamren first came to the Eugene area with her boyfriend to farm-sit for Chuck's brother Ken Kesey (who, among other things, wrote the novel *One Flew over the Cuckoo's Nest*). In 1969, after the farm sitting was over and Nancy had decided to stay in the area, she found a job working for Chuck and Sue as a bookkeeper. Nancy had been inspired by her grandmother's passion for yogurt and was eager to share and learn about dairy fermentation.

By 1970, Springfield Creamery had become the first company in the United States to sell yogurt made with, and labeled as containing, probiotic bacteria. Fortunately, their timing was good and they found eager customers in health food stores, small food co-ops, and the like. When loyal local customers would call the creamery, they were usually greeted by Nancy on the phone and simply began calling the yogurt "Nancy's yogurt." It stuck.

Fast-forward 50 years and Nancy's probiotic lineup consists of organic and natural cottage cheese, sour cream, kefir, a variety of yogurt styles, and even two plant-based ferments: oat milk nondairy yogurt and organic soy yogurt. They all contain blends of fermentation and probiotic bacterial strains, many of which are custom strains selected by Nancy and Chuck, making them unique to Nancy's delicious products. Sue (company CFO) and Chuck (company president), along with their son, daughter, and two grandsons, are still running the company. For more about the fascinating history of the company, check out their website (see Resources).

Dairy-Free Culture Sources

Here are a few of the options for dairy-free cultures. I prefer the ones with the most variety for the probiotics and flavor potential.

COMPANY	CULTURE NAME OR CLASSIFICATION	CONTAINS
Belle + Bella	Nondairy yogurt starter	*Streptococcus thermophilus, Lactobacillus delbrueckii* ssp. *bulgaricus, Lb. acidophilus*
Cultures for Health	Vegan yogurt starter	*Bifidobacterium bifidum, Lactobacillus acidophilus, Lb. casei, Lb. delbrueckii* ssp. *bulgaricus, Lb. rhamnosus, Streptococcus thermophilus*
Eugurt	Nondairy yogurt starter	*Lactobacillus* spp., *Streptococcus thermophilus, Bifidobacterium bifidum*
GetCulture/Dairy Connection	Dairy-free yogurt culture	*Bifidobacterium bifidum, B. lactis, Lactobacillus acidophilus, Lb. casei, Lb. delbrueckii* ssp. *bulgaricus, Lb. rhamnosus, Streptococcus thermophilus*

FERMENTER'S TIP

To Use or Not to Use Probiotic Capsules

Probiotic capsules from the drugstore contain different blends of bacteria proven to have health benefits, but they don't necessarily contain the strains that are best for fermentation. *Lactobacillus bulgaricus* is one of the primary yogurt bacteria, but you won't find it in most, if any, probiotic supplements. You might recall that *Lb. bulgaricus* works in a very balanced fashion with *Streptococcus thermophilus* in order to acidify the milk. *S. thermophilus* is found in many supplements, but since it's without its partner, the cultures in the capsule might not properly ferment the milk. In addition, the plethora of other probiotics found in many supplements are often never found in yogurt or kefir cultures. They won't hurt you if you use them, but the acid and flavor profile might be a surprise. When I tested a couple in coconut yogurt, I found the flavor to be quite off-putting.

Coconut Cream Yogurt
(Vegan)

Coconut milk and cream contain natural sugar, but not enough to feed the fermentation microbes and produce the desired level of tartness, so you need to add table sugar. When I didn't add sugar in my experiments, the pH only dropped to about 5.2, which is about 10 times less zippy than dairy yogurt. Even with the added sugar in this recipe, which brings the pH to the same level as dairy yogurt, the yogurt will still not taste as tart as dairy yogurt due to the wonderfully sweet flavor and richness of coconut. Commercial coconut yogurts include a bit of citric acid to add a tart flavor. If you want to try this, dissolve a pinch (no more — it is quite strong) of citric acid in the mix before fermenting.

To make coconut yogurt thick, you have two choices: you can use the thickest coconut milk product you can find (like coconut cream), or you can add thickeners. You can experiment with any variation of this combination to achieve the thickness you prefer.

Makes 2 cups

INGREDIENTS

- 1 (13.5-ounce) can coconut milk
- 1 (5.4-ounce) can coconut cream
- 1 tablespoon tapioca starch
- ½ teaspoon sugar
- ¼ teaspoon nondairy yogurt culture

STEPS

1. Combine the coconut milk, coconut cream, tapioca starch, and sugar in a medium saucepan and whisk until well blended.

2. Place the pan over medium heat and warm to 140°F (60°C), stirring constantly. Remove from the heat and let cool to 120°F (49°C).

3. Sprinkle the culture on top of the warm coconut mixture and let sit for 1 minute, then whisk it in.

4. Incubate at 110°F (43°C) for 8 hours. Chill before serving. Store in the refrigerator and use within 7 to 10 days.

Almond Kinda-Kefir from Grains

Milk kefir grains will ferment plant milks as long as you rehabilitate them with real dairy milk in between uses. Because the grains are fed dairy milk, this recipe isn't strictly vegan, but it should be fine for those with dairy allergies. Almond milk is high in protein but very low in sugar, so some sugar must be added to get the nice tang associated with kefir. Since kefir is drinkable, you won't need to add thickeners. Fresh almond milk (see the recipe on page 121) works best, but store-bought works, too. After about 16 hours of fermentation, the flavor is mildly tart and quite tasty. I actually prefer it to unfermented almond milk. This method of using grains and a bit of sugar works well with other plant milks, too.

Makes 2 cups

INGREDIENTS

2 cups plain, unsweetened almond milk

1 teaspoon sugar

1–2 teaspoons rinsed kefir grains

STEPS

1. Warm the milk to 90°F (32°C). You can gently heat the milk in a pan on the stove and then pour it into the incubation jar, or you can pour the cool milk into the incubation jar and then set the jar in a bowl of warm water to warm.

2. Add the sugar and stir until it is dissolved, then add the kefir grains. Cover and ferment at room temperature (70°F to 75°F/21°C to 24°C) for 16 to 24 hours.

3. Remove the grains, rinse, and place in a jar with fresh dairy milk to feed them. Chill the kefir before serving. Store in the refrigerator and use within 7 to 10 days.

chapter 8

Cultured Butters, Cultured Creams, and Yogurt and Kefir Cheeses

In yogurt's native lands, cultured butters and creams made from yogurt and other traditional milk ferments are common. In the United States, though, it's a pretty novel concept. Now that I've been making butter and creams this way for a while, I can't imagine not using probiotic cultures, and I've given you my favorite recipes here. This chapter also includes recipes for both soft and firm probiotic cheeses. When I am making a firm cheese, such as feta or farmhouse cheese, I like to stick with yogurt or cultured kefir rather than kefir from grains. It is a matter of taste, but traditional kefir grains include some rather pronounced yeast and acetic notes, which might be not as pleasant in the cheese as they are in the beverage. You might even get some holes in the cheese due to gas production by the yeasts, but they are only of aesthetic concern. Yogurt and kefir cultures work equally well, but the yogurt cultures work much more quickly.

Yogurt or Kefir Fromage Blanc or Chèvre

In the United States, the term *chèvre* refers to fresh goat's milk cheese. Fromage blanc is made using the same recipe as chèvre, but with cow's milk. Both are long-set, acid-coagulated cheeses with a touch of rennet (a bit more than in the skyr recipe on page 87). The resulting curd is drained to a texture ranging from dry and crumbly to slightly wet and spreadable. Both varieties are salted and are great with herbs and spices mixed in. You will need cheesecloth for this recipe.

Makes 1–2 quarts

INGREDIENTS

- 1 gallon pasteurized or high-quality raw milk
- ⅛ teaspoon powdered yogurt or kefir culture or ⅛ cup fresh yogurt or kefir

- 1 drop (0.05 ml) double-strength or 2 drops (0.1 ml) single-strength rennet diluted just before use in 4 tablespoons cool, nonchlorinated water
- 1 teaspoon salt, or to taste

STEPS

1. Heat the milk to 110°F (43°C) if you are using yogurt culture or to 95°F (35°C) if you are using kefir culture.

2. Add the culture. If using powdered culture, sprinkle it on top of the milk and let sit for 1 minute, then whisk it in. If using fresh yogurt or kefir, combine the yogurt or kefir with ¼ cup of the warm milk in a small bowl and whisk until smooth, then add the mixture to the rest of the milk.

3. Stir in the diluted rennet.

4. Incubate at 110°F (43°C) for the yogurt version or at 95°F (35°C) for the kefir version for 8 to 12 hours, or until about ¼ inch of whey covers the curd and the sides are pulling away from the container.

5. Line a colander with cheesecloth and pour boiling water over both to sanitize. Spoon or pour the hot curd into the colander, cover, and let drain, stirring occasionally, until the cheese reaches the desired texture, 4 to 6 hours.

6. Turn the cheese into a container and mix in the salt. Refrigerate for a few days before serving to improve the flavor.

Yogurt or Kefir Butter

Hand-churned butter is a true delight, both in its simplicity and in its epicurean enchantment. Butter is made by warming cream to room temperature and then agitating it. When warm, the fat globules in the cream soften. When the agitation causes them to smash into each other, they will stick together, eventually forming a mass of butter and leaving behind a low-fat liquid — the buttermilk.

This recipe calls for adding kefir or yogurt cultures to the cream to make cultured butter. Cultured butter is only slightly tangy and has wonderful layers of flavor, depending on the variety of starter bacteria used. If you are using a yogurt culture, choose one that doesn't create very viscous results, as these are much harder to agitate properly. If you are using kefir grains, use light cream or even half-and-half instead of heavy cream — it will be much easier to remove the grains from one of these thinner liquids. You don't need a butter churn to make butter; a glass quart jar will do just fine.

Makes about 1 cup

INGREDIENTS

   2 cups cream (heavy or light)
   ⅛ teaspoon yogurt or kefir culture,
        ⅛ cup fresh yogurt or cultured kefir,
        or 2 tablespoons kefir grains

   ¼ teaspoon salt (optional)
        Seasonings to taste, such as
        herbes de Provence, tarragon,
        saffron, smoked salt, or roasted
        garlic (optional)

STEPS

1. Pour the cream into a glass quart jar or butter churn. Add the culture and stir to mix it in.

2. If you are using yogurt culture, incubate at 110°F (43°C) for 4 to 6 hours, then cool to 68°F to 72°F (20°C to 22°C). If you are using kefir culture, incubate at 68°F to 72°F (20°C to 22°C) for 18 hours.

3. Shake the jar or churn the butter until the butter and buttermilk separate. If you are shaking a jar, be sure not to overwarm the cream by holding the jar portion in your warm hands. Instead, grip the lid portion and shake the jar sharply up and down. This step could take anywhere from a few seconds to 10 minutes, depending on your technique and the amount of fat in the cream.

Recipe continues on next page

Yogurt or Kefir Butter continued

4. Drain off the buttermilk. You can save it for drinking or use it to make delicious biscuits, pancakes, and waffles. Prepare a large bowl of ice water.

5. Remove the glob of wet butter from the jar or churn and place it in a medium bowl. Set the bowl in the bowl of ice water and, using a large spoon, work the butter with the back of the spoon, gently pressing out and draining excess moisture.

6. When very little moisture remains, blend in the salt, if using. If you want to flavor the butter, add the seasonings now as well.

7. Work the butter a bit longer, or use a butter press to remove as much moisture as possible. The less moisture in the butter, the longer its shelf life, the better its texture when frozen, and the less likely it will be to splatter when cooking.

8. Press the butter into a butter bell or tub. If you have used a butter press, then the formed butter can be wrapped in parchment or waxed paper. Depending on how much moisture is in the butter, it should keep for many weeks, or even months, in the refrigerator, and indefinitely in the freezer.

Real Buttermilk

The translucent liquid and little droplets of moisture that you drain and work from your freshly churned butter are real buttermilk. Most of us are familiar with cultured buttermilk, but real buttermilk is quite different. It's a bit like whey but has more solids and, of course, little fresh butter freckles throughout. When squeezed from fresh cream butter, not cultured butter, it is sweet and simple, but when collected from cultured butter it is complex, nourishing, and delicious. So don't forget to save the buttermilk when you make yogurt or kefir butter — it's simply amazing! In fact, I can rarely even wait to chill it before drinking it. It's the reward for all that effort of churning.

Yogurt or Kefir Ricotta

The word *ricotta* literally means "re-cooked." Cheesemaking produces a lot of whey (up to 90 percent of the original milk volume), which contains a lot of whey proteins. When that slightly acidic whey is heated to 180°F (82°C) or a bit higher, those proteins spontaneously curdle and float to the top. The traditional ricotta maker then scoops out those curds and drains them. In this way, traditional ricotta is a by-product of making Italian cheeses such as mozzarella.

We'll use plain kefir or yogurt as the acid source to curdle hot milk. The resulting ricotta is much more interesting than whole-milk ricotta, thanks to the flavor of the kefir or yogurt. This is a great use for older yogurt or kefir that is not only more acidic and will curdle the milk more readily but that has already lost a good deal of its probiotic potential. You'll need cheesecloth for this recipe.

Makes about 2 cups

INGREDIENTS

4 cups milk

2 cups yogurt or kefir
   (cultured or from grains)

¼–½ teaspoon salt (optional)

STEPS

1. Pour the milk into a large stainless-steel pot and set it over medium-high heat. Heat to boiling, constantly scraping the bottom with a spatula so the milk doesn't stick and scorch. Cool to about 195°F (91°C).

2. Gently stir in the yogurt or kefir. You will see the curds form instantly, and the clear whey will begin to separate.

3. Line a colander with cheesecloth and place it over the sink or another pot. Scoop, ladle, or pour the hot whey and curd into the colander. Let the curd drain for about 10 minutes, or until it reaches the desired texture. Every few minutes, gently lift two sides of the cloth and tip the curd back and forth to encourage draining.

4. Mix in the salt, if using, then transfer the curd to a container and cool in the refrigerator. Use within 1 week or freeze.

Whipped Yogurt or Kefir Crème Fraîche

Crème fraîche is simply sour cream's more decadent cousin. The fat content of sour cream is regulated in the United States to about 18 percent, while the fat content of crème fraîche can vary but is usually closer to that of light cream (20 percent). I make mine with heavy whipping cream (about 37 percent fat) and have no regrets! This recipe is great for desserts of all kinds.

The whipping process demonstrates the amazing effect that temperature has on the milk fat globule. Since the cream is agitated when cold, the fat globules will not stick together (as opposed to when you make butter with warm cream). Instead, air is incorporated into the cream, doubling the volume and creating whipped cream. Cultured heavy cream usually whips into a very thick product. If you don't want it that thick, use a lighter cream or add about ¼ cup milk to the heavy cream.

Makes 2 cups

INGREDIENTS

- 2 cups cream (heavy or light)
- ⅛ teaspoon powdered yogurt or kefir culture or ⅛ cup fresh yogurt or cultured kefir
- ¼ teaspoon salt (optional)
- 2 teaspoons sugar or maple syrup (optional)

STEPS

1. Pour the cream into a glass quart jar. Add the culture and stir to mix it in.

2. If you are using yogurt culture, incubate at 110°F (43°C) for 1 to 2 hours, then cool to 68°F to 72°F (20°C to 22°C). If you are using kefir culture, incubate at 68°F to 72°F (20°C to 22°C) for 4 to 8 hours.

3. Place the cultured cream in the refrigerator or in an ice water bath until cold, between 35°F and 40°F (2°C and 4°C).

4. Pour the cultured cream into a bowl. Mix in the salt and sugar, if using. Using a whisk or a hand mixer, beat until stiff peaks form. The whipped crème fraîche will keep in the refrigerator, without losing its texture, for several days.

Whipped Yogurt
Crème Fraîche
(page 136)

Yogurt Ricotta
(page 135)

Yogurt
Sour Cream

Yogurt or Kefir Sour Cream

Commercial sour cream is made from milk that contains about 18 percent butterfat (for comparison, half-and-half is about 12 percent butterfat, light cream about 20 percent, and whipping or heavy cream 35 to 38 percent). For this recipe, I prefer using half-and-half to create an incredibly rich and thick sour cream. Many commercial sour creams include quite an array of additives, from thickeners to flavoring agents. You'll be amazed at how easy, and superior, this sour cream is!

Whether to use yogurt or kefir culture will depend simply on which cultures you have and how much time you have. The yogurt version is much faster. If you use kefir grains, note that they are a bit of a challenge to fish out of the thickened cream. This is our go-to sour cream now, and we get probiotics with every rich dollop.

Makes 1 quart

INGREDIENTS

1 quart half-and-half

⅛ teaspoon yogurt or kefir culture, ⅛ cup fresh yogurt or cultured kefir, or 2 tablespoons kefir grains

STEPS

1. Pour the half-and-half into a glass quart jar. Add the culture and stir to mix it in.

2. If you are using yogurt culture, incubate at 110°F (43°C) for 8 to 12 hours, then cool to between 68°F and 72°F (20°C and 22°C) and hold the cream there for 4 to 6 hours longer. If you are using kefir culture, incubate at about 75°F (24°C) for 24 hours. Chill before serving. Store the sour cream in the refrigerator; it will remain fresh tasting for 2 to 3 weeks.

Quick Yogurt Mozzarella

The traditional process of making mozzarella is an all-day affair that, while gratifying, requires more dedication than many of us have time for. Quick, 30-minute mozzarella was popularized by my mentor and hero Ricki Carroll in her seminal book *Home Cheese Making*. The trick is to add a precise amount of citric acid, which makes the milk plasticize and stretch when heat is applied. Here we'll use yogurt along with a bit of citric acid to create a fresh mozzarella with almost as much flavor as traditional, long-process curds.

As with all of the quick mozzarella recipes, there is a risk of adding too much or too little acid to the milk. The goal pH, if you are able to check it, is between 5.1 and 5.2. Depending upon the acidity of the milk, you might miss this target. To help reduce this risk, be sure to measure the yogurt carefully. Use undrained yogurt that has a tart, but not too sour, flavor. I don't recommend kefir for this recipe as it is usually more acidic than yogurt and might drop the pH too low. If your curd won't stretch and is rubbery and firm, add a bit more citric acid next time. If it starts to stretch and then falls apart, add less. You'll need a thermometer, cheesecloth, a long knife, and gloves for handling the hot curd.

Makes approximately 1 pound

Tips for Working Mozzarella Curd

- Pull and stretch the curd only when it gives easily; reheat as soon as resistance is firm.

- Pull and refold the curd in the same direction each time to help the protein strands elongate.

- If you are forming the curd into balls, work the curd by gently pressing your thumbs around the sides in a circular motion that pushes the sides into the center back (similar to forming a loaf of bread dough).

- Remember, less is more! Fats and tenderness will be lost from overworking.

INGREDIENTS

- 1 gallon whole milk (not ultra-pasteurized)
- ½ cup fresh plain yogurt
- 1¼ teaspoon citric acid diluted in ⅛ cup cool water
- ¼ teaspoon double-strength or ¼ teaspoon single-strength rennet diluted just before use in ⅛ cup cool, nonchlorinated water
- 2 teaspoons salt

STEPS

1. Combine the milk and yogurt in a 5- or 6-quart pot and whisk until well blended. Stir in the diluted citric acid.

2. Place the milk pot inside a larger pot, and fill the larger pot with enough water to come up the sides of the inner pot. Set over medium heat and warm the milk, stirring gently, to 95°F (35°C). Remove from the heat but leave in the water bath.

3. Hold a slotted spoon or cheese ladle over the milk and pour the diluted rennet through the spoon into the milk (the spoon helps disperse it). Use the slotted spoon to stir the milk with five to seven up-and-down strokes, then hold it to the top of the milk in several spots to help still the milk. Cover the milk and let sit undisturbed for 5 minutes.

4. Using a long knife, cut the curd into approximately ¼-inch cubes by first cutting vertical columns and then making horizontal cuts, angled down, through the curd mass. Note that it's impossible to get actual cubes! Just do your best and average the size. Let rest for 5 minutes longer. The curds will have a spongy, soft texture and will likely become very small during stirring.

5. Gently stir the curds with a rubber spatula. Then place the pot in its water bath setup over low heat and heat to 105°F (41°C). (The temperature will have already increased somewhat from the residual heat in the water bath.)

6. Line a colander with cheesecloth and place over a bowl. Pour the warm curds into the cloth. Use the cheesecloth to flip the curds over a couple of times to allow them to drain more. You don't need to keep them warm.

7. Pour the whey back into the pot and add 1 teaspoon of the salt. Set over medium heat and heat to 130°F (54°C). Fill a large bowl half full of cool water.

STEP 4

Recipe continues on next page

8. Stir the remaining 1 teaspoon salt into the whey. Cut a small piece of curd and immerse it in the hot whey for about 30 seconds. Pull at the curd to see if it stretches. If necessary, you can increase the whey temperature up to 150°F (66°C) to help the curd stretch.

9. Gently work the curd (see the tips on page 140), reheating as needed. It's very easy to overwork it and squeeze out the butterfat, turning it into rubbery balls, so be gentle!

10. Once the mozzarella has taken shape, place it in the cool water bath. Quick mozzarella is best eaten just after making, when it's at its tenderest. However, it can be firmed up in the fridge for a few days for use as a melting cheese for pizza and the like. Once made, it should be used within about 1 week.

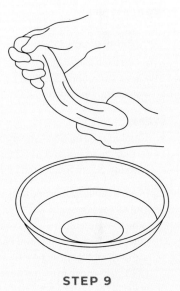

STEP 9

CHEESEMAKER'S TIP
What Is Cheese Salt?

At classes, I'm often asked, "What is cheese salt?" The short answer is, "There is no such thing!" When making cheese, salt is used for two reasons: to add flavor and to help preserve the cheese. In some cases, such as cheeses meant to be eaten immediately like ricotta and quick mozzarella, the salt is there just to add flavor. For those cheeses that utilize starter bacteria to help create flavor over time, it's important to use only pure salt, because additives, such as iodine, can harm the microbes. You can buy pure sodium chloride at any grocery store. Look for a fine salt. Sea salt is a great choice.

Yogurt or Kefir Feta

If you want to start making more complex cheeses, feta is a great place to start. It can be enjoyed fresh or aged in the refrigerator, and it takes very few supplies to make it. Whether or not it is due to my Greek heritage and childhood of enjoying feta I can't say, but I am picky about feta. Most commercial American feta is not made with the craftsmanship the cheese deserves. Once you get comfortable with this recipe, set a batch aside for aging and see the marvelous wonders that time can work on cheese. You'll need a thermometer, cheesecloth, and a long knife for this recipe.

Makes 1½–2 pounds

INGREDIENTS

- 2 gallons whole milk
- ¼ teaspoon powdered yogurt or kefir culture or ¼ cup fresh yogurt or kefir
- ⅛ teaspoon calcium chloride diluted in 2 tablespoons cool water (optional; suggested for store-bought, homogenized milk)
- ⅛ teaspoon double-strength or ¼ teaspoon single-strength rennet diluted just before use in ¼ cup cool, nonchlorinated water
- 2 tablespoons pure salt (such as sea salt or any noniodized salt with no added anticaking agents)

STEPS

1. Pour the milk into a large pot and place that pot inside a larger pot. Fill the larger pot with enough water to come up the sides of the inner pot. Set over low to medium heat and warm the milk to between 88°F and 90°F (31°C and 32°C). The water in the outer pot will be hotter than the milk, so either turn the heat off before the milk reaches its goal or be ready to remove the milk pot from the water bath.

2. Add the culture. If using powdered culture, sprinkle it on top of the milk and let sit for 3 to 5 minutes, then stir gently for 2 to 5 minutes. If using fresh yogurt or kefir, combine the yogurt or kefir with ½ cup of the warm milk in a small bowl and whisk, then add the mixture to the rest of the milk.

3. If you are using yogurt culture, incubate at 105°F (41°C), stirring occasionally, for 1 hour. If you are using kefir culture, incubate at 88°F to 90°F (31°C to 32°C), stirring occasionally, for 1 hour. You can usually accomplish this by covering the milk pot and letting it sit in the water bath. Stir in the diluted calcium chloride, if using.

Recipe continues on next page

4. Using a slotted spoon or cheese ladle, stir the milk using an up-and-down motion for a few strokes. Hold the ladle over the milk and pour the diluted rennet over it and into the milk. Stir for 1 minute longer, then hold the ladle to the top of the milk in several spots to help still the milk.

5. Cover the pot and let sit undisturbed until a clean break is achieved; that will be 25 to 30 minutes if you are using yogurt culture and about 45 minutes if you are using kefir culture.

STEP 5

6. Using a long knife, cut the curds into ½-inch columns. With your blade at an angle, make a few horizontal cuts through the columns. Cover and let rest for 10 minutes to allow the curds to firm up a bit.

STEP 6

7. Gently stir the curds just enough to move them slowly in the pot. Check the temperature. If the yogurt-cultured mixture is not 105°F to 110°F (41°C to 43°C) or if the kefir-cultured mixture is not 88°F to 90° (31°C to 32°C), return the pot in its hot water bath setup to the stovetop and reheat to that temperature. Continue to stir for a total of 20 minutes. The curds will shrink and firm up a bit during this time.

8. Line a colander with cheesecloth and slowly pour the curds into the cloth. Let drain for a few minutes. Alternatively, the curd can be drained in a basket form (as in photo on page 144).

9. Gather the corners of the cloth into a knot and loop a shoelace or string through the knot. Hang the draining cheese over a pot and allow to drain for 18 hours at room temperature. If using a form, flip the wheel twice over the 18 hours.

10. Remove the cheese from the cloth and slice into 1-inch slabs. Stack in layers in a small container or ziplock bag, and cover all sides with the salt. Cover and place in the fridge.

11. Allow the cheese to lightly age and mellow for a few days. Turn the slabs daily to allow the collecting salty whey (brine) to coat each slice. You can age feta for months in the fridge as long as it is fully submerged in the brine and the air space is filled or covered to the level of the whey with plastic film. If air is touching the brine and/or cheese, harmless but unsightly molds will develop.

Farmhouse Wheel

The term *farmhouse* has no strict definition in the cheesemaking world. It's meant to evoke thoughts of small handmade batches, and this recipe certainly fits that bill! I like to use this recipe to introduce the technique of making pressed cheese. Not only is this cheese fairly simple to make (compared to a traditional cheddar), but it also lends itself to added flavors and some brief aging to improve the flavor. If you decide you want to age it longer, you'll need to read up on aging options for the home cheesemaker (see the resources section). You'll need a thermometer, cheesecloth, a long knife, a cheese form with a follower, a water jug or other weight for pressing, and a large tub with a lid for this recipe.

Makes approximately one 2-pound wheel

INGREDIENTS

- 2 gallons whole milk
- ¼ teaspoon powdered yogurt or kefir culture or ¼ cup fresh yogurt or kefir
- ¼ teaspoon calcium chloride diluted in ¼ cup cool water (optional; suggested for store-bought, homogenized milk)
- 2 teaspoons hot pepper flakes or lavender buds, or a few drops of truffle oil (optional)

- ⅛ teaspoon double-strength or ¼ teaspoon single-strength rennet diluted just before use in ¼ cup cool, nonchlorinated water
- 2 tablespoon pure salt (such as sea salt or any noniodized salt with no added anticaking agents)

STEPS

1. Pour the milk into a large pot, and place that pot inside a larger pot. Fill the larger pot with enough water to come up the sides of the inner pot. Set over low to medium heat and warm the milk to 88°F to 90°F (31°C to 32°C). The water in the outer pot will be hotter than the milk, so either turn the heat off before the milk reaches its goal or be ready to remove the milk pot from the water bath.

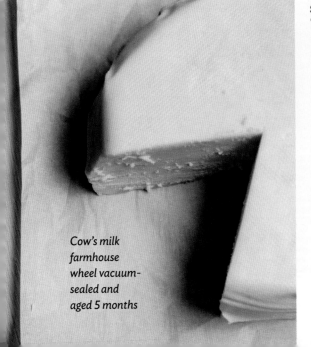

Cow's milk farmhouse wheel vacuum-sealed and aged 5 months

2. Add the culture. If using powdered culture, sprinkle it on top of the milk and let sit for 3 to 5 minutes, then stir gently for 2 to 5 minutes. If using fresh yogurt or kefir, combine the yogurt or kefir with ½ cup of the warm milk in a small bowl and whisk to combine, then add the mixture to the rest of the milk.

3. Stir in the diluted calcium chloride, if using.

4. If you are using yogurt culture, incubate at 105°F (41°C), stirring occasionally, for 1 hour. If you are using kefir culture, incubate at 88°F to 90°F (31°C to 32°C), stirring occasionally, for 1 hour. You can usually accomplish this by covering the pot and letting it sit in the water bath.

5. If you are adding dried herbs, simmer them in 1 cup water for 5 minutes to soften. Strain and add the liquid only to the milk (you'll add the herbs later). If you are adding truffle oil or any other liquid flavoring, add it now.

6. Using a ladle, stir the milk using an up-and-down motion for about 1 minute. Hold the ladle over the milk and pour the diluted rennet over it and into the milk. Stir for 1 minute longer, then hold the ladle to the top of the milk in several spots to help still the milk.

7. Cover and let the milk sit undisturbed, maintaining the temperature at 102°F to 105°F (39°C to 41°C) if using yogurt culture or at 88°F to 90°F (31°C to 32°C) if using kefir culture until a clean break is achieved, about 45 minutes. You can usually maintain the temperature by covering the pot and leaving it in the water bath. If it cools off during this phase, don't try to rewarm it until step 9.

8. Using a long knife, cut the curds into columns. With your blade at an angle, make a few horizontal cuts about ⅜ inches apart through the columns to make cubes. Then let the curds rest for 5 minutes.

9. Heat the curds gradually, over the course of 30 minutes, stirring gently, to 110°F (43°C) if using yogurt culture or 100°F (38°C) if using kefir culture; increase the temperature very slowly during the first 15 minutes. If needed, cut any large curds into smaller pieces during stirring. Hold at that temperature (110°F/43°C if using yogurt culture, or 100°F/38°C if using kefir culture), stirring gently, for 20 minutes. The curds will shrink and become slightly springy — a bit like a hard-boiled egg white.

10. Remove the pot from the heat and let the curds set for 5 minutes.

11. Line a colander with cheesecloth and place over a bowl. Pour the curds into the colander. Save the

Recipe continues on next page

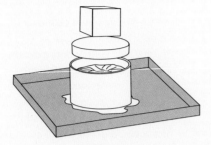

STEP 12

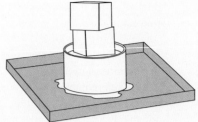

STEP 14

whey for later use. Stir the softened herbs, if using, into the curds.

12. Place the cheese form on a tray or a drain board. Lift the bundle of curds from the colander and lower into the form. Hand-press the curds into the bottom and pack as tightly as you can. Fold the cloth over the top and add the follower. Place about 1 pound of weight on top. Let press for 15 minutes. All pressing stages are best done at warm room temperature (about 85°F/29°C). You can cover the wheel while it is being pressed with a large tub and then put towels over that to help keep it warm.

13. Remove the weight and the follower. Remove the wrapped cheese from the form, unwrap it, and flip it over. Rearrange the cheesecloth in the form, and then replace the cheese, pressing the cloth into the form along with it; the cheese should still look a bit wrinkled and the rind not yet smooth. Set the follower and the 1-pound weight back in place and press for 30 minutes.

14. Repeat step 13. This time the rind should be smoother but still not evenly closed. Add another 1 pound of weight for a total of 2 pounds. Now press for 60 minutes.

15. Repeat step 13 again. Now the rind should be very even, perhaps with a few small openings. If not, you may add up to 2 pounds more weight. Now press for 4 hours.

16. Remove the cheese from the form, cut off a tiny piece, and taste it. It should have a very mild tang and taste milky with a hint of buttermilk or yogurt. If it isn't slightly tangy, press it for 1 hour longer and taste it again. If you are checking pH, the goal is 5.2 to 5.4.

17. When you have achieved the desired tang, take the cheese from the form, unwrap it, and rub the cheese all over with 1 tablespoon of the salt. Return the cheese to the form, without the cheesecloth, weight, or follower, and let it set for 30 minutes.

18. Remove the cheese from the form and rub it with the remaining 1 tablespoon salt. Place the cheese in a tub, put on the lid, and let it set in the refrigerator for 8 to 12 hours. After this initial setting, there may be some salty whey at the bottom of the tub; if so, rub the whey all over the cheese and flip it over.

19. Continue to age the cheese in the refrigerator for 3 more days, flipping it and rubbing whey over it as needed two or three times a day. During this time the texture and flavor of the cheese will change as the salt moves through the wheel and the cheese mellows.

20. Pat the cheese dry with paper towels and wrap tightly in plastic wrap or a plastic bag. Store in the refrigerator for up to 4 weeks. It will last longer and even age if there is very little air in the container. If a little mold develops on the outside, either cut it off before eating the cheese or rub it with a bit of vinegar to remove it. Alternatively, vacuum seal and age in the refrigerator for several months to develop flavor and character.

The Chemistry of Acid and Heat

One of the simplest ways to make cheese is to utilize heat and acid to curdle the milk. In fresh milk, the milk proteins stay suspended in the liquid by literally repelling each other. They have an overall negative charge, and if you recall playing with magnets as a kid (or more recently), you'll remember that like repels like — that is, negative charges repel each other. You might also recall from school science that heat excites molecules, making them easier to alter. When you heat the milk and add acid, which, simply put, has a positive electrical charge, you alter the milk proteins, making them clump together. The hotter the milk, the less acid you need. Typically, a cheesemaker will use vinegar or diluted citric acid to cause the curdling, but tart kefir or yogurt is also a great acid source.

Can You Use Ultra-pasteurized Milk?

According to many cheese- and yogurt-making books, blogs, and articles, you should never use ultra-pasteurized milk. This isn't always true! A quick review: When milk is heated beyond 135°F (57°C), some changes start to happen that really matter to the cheesemaker. The longer the milk is held warm, the more whey proteins are altered. Instead of staying in the liquid part of the milk, they start sticking to the cheese proteins. If you are making a rennet-coagulated cheese, the sticky whey proteins basically block the rennet from doing its job. The result is a weak, pasty curd. However, and that's a big however, if you are making an acid-coagulated product such as yogurt, kefir, ricotta, or fromage blanc, it doesn't matter at all! In fact, we regularly use high heat to purposefully alter, or denature, those whey proteins to improve the texture and protein content of yogurt. So feel free to use ultra-pasteurized milk in your acid-coagulated dairy ferments and cheeses that don't use any rennet.

Quick 'n' Squeaky Curds

Fresh, squeaky cheddar curds are one of the most fun cheesy things to eat. Traditional recipes, however, take most of the day to make. I came up with this recipe as a way to shave off a few hours and still have great results. I use yogurt and adore the fresh, unique flavor and the texture. Try your fresh curds plain, with pesto, with caramelized garlic, or even as poutine — that north-of-the-border treat of French fries topped with cheese curds and drenched in brown gravy — or even deep-fried curds (pictured in Really Ranch Dressing on page 172). Yum! You will need a thermometer, a long knife, and a colander for this recipe.

Makes about ¼ pound

INGREDIENTS

- 1 gallon whole milk
- 1 cup fresh yogurt or kefir
- ⅛ teaspoon calcium chloride diluted in 2 tablespoons cool water (optional; suggested for store-bought, homogenized milk)
- ¼ teaspoon double-strength or ½ teaspoon single-strength rennet diluted just before use in ⅛ cup cool, nonchlorinated water
- 1 teaspoon salt

STEPS

1. Pour the milk into a large pot, and place that pot inside a larger pot. Fill the larger pot with enough water to come up the sides of the inner pot. Set over low to medium heat and warm the milk to 95°F (35°C).

2. Combine the yogurt or kefir with 1 cup of the warm milk in a small bowl and whisk together, then add the mixture to the rest of the milk. It's okay if the milk cools to 93°F (34°C) or so. Stir in the diluted calcium chloride, if using.

3. Hold a slotted spoon or cheese ladle over the milk and pour the diluted rennet through the spoon into the milk (the spoon helps disperse it). Then use the ladle to stir the milk with five up-and-down strokes. Hold the ladle to the top of the milk in several spots to help still the milk.

4. Cover the milk and let sit undisturbed, maintaining the temperature between 93°F and 95°F (34°C and 35°C) until it coagulates, 30 to 45 minutes. Test the curd for a clean break (see the illustration on page 146, step 6). Note: If it cools off during this phase, don't try to rewarm it until step 9.

Recipe continues on page 155

Quick 'n' Squeaky Curds *continued*

5. Using a long knife, cut the curd mass into ⅜- to ¼-inch columns, then with your blade at an angle, make a few horizontal cuts about ⅜ inch apart through the columns. Let rest for 5 minutes.

6. Maintaining the temperature at 95°F (35°C), stir the curds very gently for 5 minutes. Then warm the curds to 110°F (43°C) by increasing the heat very slowly over 30 minutes.

7. Line a colander with cheesecloth and place over a bowl. Heat a pot of water to about 120°F (49°C).

8. Pour the curds into the colander and tie the cloth in a bundle. Set the colander and bundle over the pot of warm water to help keep the curds between 102°F and 105°F (39°C and 41°C). Cover the pot with a lid if needed. Let sit for 15 minutes.

9. Open the bundle and cut the curd ball in half. Line the colander with the cheesecloth. Stack the curd halves on top of each other and place back in the cloth-lined colander. Fill a plastic ziplock bag with 110°F (43°C) hot water and set on top of the curds. This helps keep the curd slabs warm and create the desired texture. Let sit for 15 minutes.

10. Uncover and rotate the two curd slabs and re-cover with the bag of hot water. Let sit for 15 minutes longer. Repeat rotating and warming the curd slabs until they have the texture of cooked chicken breast, about 1 hour.

11. Cut the slabs into pieces that are ½ to 1 inch by ¼ to ½ inch.

12. Set the colander over the pot of hot water. Place the curd pieces in the colander and sprinkle with ½ teaspoon of the salt. Stir, then cover with the hot water bag, rewarming as needed, and let sit for 5 minutes. This step is called mellowing.

13. Repeat the salting and mellowing one more time. Eat the curds right away, or refrigerate for up to 3 weeks, but they lose their squeakiness within the first day.

Working with Homogenized Milk

Fresh, whole nonhomogenized milk is always your best choice for cheesemaking because homogenization restructures the milk fat in a way that interferes with rennet coagulation. However, unless you have your own dairy animals, nonhomogenized, or cream-top, milk can be hard to find and is also quite expensive. If homogenized milk is your best option, you can get pretty good results if you adapt your recipe as follows:

- For firm rennet-set cheeses such as feta (page 145), farmhouse wheel (page 148), and squeaky curds (page 153), add liquid calcium chloride solution (32 to 33 percent concentration, purchased from a cheesemaking supply company) at a rate of ⅛ teaspoon per gallon of milk. While calcium chloride doesn't strictly solve the issues of homogenization, it does help create a firmer curd when using milk that has been sitting around on the supply chain shelf for a while, which all homogenized milk has been.

- After cutting the curds, allow them to sit and "heal" for twice as long as the recipe recommends before stirring them.

- Be very gentle when stirring the curds. You may even need to just rock the pot back and forth for the initial stirring. Even when you are gentle, they will gradually break into much smaller pieces. Expect this.

Probiotics in Cheese

It sounds great — just use yogurt or kefir cultures to make cheese, and voilà, probiotic cheese! Right? Well, maybe. Whether you make the cheese from raw milk or pasteurized milk with added probiotic cultures, the beneficial bacteria may not survive for long. As we've discussed, the acid environment of yogurt and kefir means that the more they age, the fewer probiotics they have. However, it's believed that the lower-acid environment of cheese (with a pH of about 5.4 compared to 4.4 in yogurt) provides a more hospitable environment for the bacteria. In fact, some strains of probiotic bacteria not only survive in aged cheese, but their numbers can actually increase!

Because of the health benefits and the marketing value of probiotic foods, more researchers are investigating which strains survive and in what numbers so that cheese producers can honestly make health benefit claims on their labels. For the sake of this book, all of the cheeses we're making are meant to be eaten fresh or after a short aging period, so you can feel fairly confident that the probiotic microbes will be alive and well when you consume the cheeses.

part three

DISHES, DRINKS, AND DELIGHTS

Saucy Salads
and Condiments

There is a long-standing cultural tradition of using yogurt and kefir as a base for cooling, healthy salads and sauces. From Greek tzatziki to Indian raita, dairy ferments are combined with many ingredients to make delicious side dishes and condiments. The recipes in this chapter might just prime your creative juices and nudge your dairy ferment fun in a whole new direction!

Classic Indian Cucumber Raita

If you love Indian food like I do, then you are familiar with creamy, refreshing raita. No Indian meal, in my opinion, is complete without a bowl of this tangy, cooling sauce flecked with bits of cucumber and spice.

Makes 4 cups

INGREDIENTS

- 4 medium cucumbers, diced
- 2 green chiles, seeded and finely diced
- 1–2 garlic cloves, finely minced or juiced
- Handful of mint leaves, finely chopped

- 2 cups plain yogurt (page 73)
- 4 teaspoons extra-virgin olive oil or ghee
- 2–4 tablespoons fresh lemon juice
- Salt and freshly ground black pepper

STEPS

1. Combine the cucumbers, chiles, garlic, and mint in a large bowl.

2. Stir in the yogurt, oil, and lemon juice, and season with salt and pepper to taste.

3. Cover and chill in the refrigerator for a few hours to improve the flavor. Before serving, stir and season as needed. Raita will keep for about 1 week in the refrigerator.

Jicama, Red Pepper, and Toasted Cumin Spicy Raita

This recipe has a south-of-the-border kick and works great with hearty Mexican-type dishes like mole and enchiladas. It's also perfect as a side dish for grilled steaks and barbecue of any kind. If you haven't used jicama before, it's a versatile root vegetable with a lovely, tender crunch and mild sweetness. It has a very tough outer skin that needs to be peeled off completely with a knife. You can substitute ground cumin for cumin seed (use about half as much), but the flavor won't be nearly as pleasing. Once you try freshly toasted cumin seed, you might never want to go back to the ground stuff!

Makes 8 cups

INGREDIENTS

- 4 cups grated jicama (from 2–3 jicamas)
- 1 red bell pepper, cut into long, thin strips
- 1–2 garlic cloves, minced or juiced
- 4 teaspoons cumin seed, dry toasted and then lightly crushed
- 1 teaspoon paprika
- 1 teaspoon red pepper flakes
- Pinch of brown sugar
- 2 cups plain yogurt (page 73)
- 2 tablespoons lime juice
- 4 teaspoons olive oil
- Handful of cilantro leaves
- Salt and freshly ground black pepper

STEPS

1. Combine the grated jicama and bell pepper strips in a large bowl.

2. Combine the garlic, 2 teaspoons of the cumin seed, the paprika, pepper flakes, sugar, yogurt, lime juice, and oil in a medium bowl. Mix well.

3. Add the yogurt and spice mixture to the vegetables, and toss, mixing well to coat thoroughly.

4. Add half of the cilantro leaves and mix well.

5. Cover the bowl and chill in the refrigerator for a few hours to improve the flavor. When you're ready to serve, stir the raita, taste again, and season to taste with salt and black pepper. Garnish with the remaining cilantro and the remaining 2 teaspoons cumin seed. Any leftover raita will keep for about 1 week in the refrigerator.

Ethiopian-Inspired Eggplant Raita

It's worth seeking out the amazing Ethiopian spice mix called berbere (see the sidebar on page 163 for more on exotic spice blends). The mixture varies but often contains coriander, nutmeg, paprika, fenugreek, allspice, clove, black pepper, and cumin. Think of it as East Africa's curry or chili powder. I love it in many dishes — including those that aren't authentically Ethiopian. If you don't have a local source, it's easy to find online. I get mine from the Teeny Tiny Spice Company.

Makes 5 cups

INGREDIENTS

- 4 tablespoons extra-virgin olive oil
- 1 large or 2 small eggplants, sliced into ½-inch rounds
- 2 cups plain yogurt (page 73)
- 1 medium shallot, minced
- ¼ cup chopped walnuts
- 1-2 garlic cloves, minced
- 2-4 teaspoons fresh lemon juice
- 1 tablespoon toasted sesame oil
- 2 teaspoons Ethiopian berbere powder or chili powder
- ¼ teaspoon red pepper flakes
- Salt and freshly ground black pepper

STEPS

1. Heat the olive oil in a skillet over medium-high heat. Add the eggplant slices and sear for about 4 minutes on each side. Let cool, then cube the seared eggplant and place in a large bowl.

2. Add the yogurt, shallot, walnuts, garlic, lemon juice, sesame oil, berbere powder, and pepper flakes, and mix well. Season to taste with salt and black pepper.

3. Cover and chill in the refrigerator for a few hours to improve the flavor. When you're ready to serve, stir and taste again, then season as needed. The raita will keep for about 1 week in the refrigerator.

Exotic Spice Blends Perfect for Dairy Ferments

Powdered spice blends are the perfect shortcut to an exotic experience. Sauces, soups, dips, and salads can all be instantly transformed with a sprinkle of the right spices. Most blends familiar to Westerners, such as curry powder and chili powder, have their roots in more authentic regional blends that would have been made from freshly pulverized herbs and spices. Since many of these blends originate in the same part of the world where yogurt and kefir have been staple foods for as long as anyone can remember, they usually pair wonderfully with dairy ferments.

Not every store will carry the best blends, however. Ubiquitous curry powder, such as what I use in the dip recipe on page 174, is wonderful, even if it isn't really Indian. If you really want to take your dishes to the next level, though, put the following blends on your grocery list. You can find them all online.

BERBERE: An Ethiopian blend that often includes spices such as paprika, black pepper, coriander, nutmeg, ginger, ajwain, allspice, chili, fenugreek, cardamom, clove, salt, onion, and garlic.

CHAAT MASALA: An Indian, Pakistani, and Bangladeshi blend that includes spices such as anardana (dried pomegranate), amchoor (mango powder), cumin, black pepper, ginger, salt, cayenne, asafetida, thyme, and peppermint. It imparts a slightly hot, tart flavor.

GARAM MASALA: An Indian subcontinent blend that includes spices such as black and white pepper, cinnamon, nutmeg or mace, cardamom, bay leaf, cumin, and coriander. It is slightly sweeter than chaat masala.

ZA'ATAR: A Middle Eastern blend that usually includes thyme, roasted sesame seeds, and sumac. It's great for dips and sprinkled over baked potatoes and veggies topped with yogurt sour cream.

If you're not ready to commit to a full order of any one of these, many companies offer variety packs with a little bit of several blends. Not only is this a great way to taste your way around the Old World, but the little tins are really cute.

Savory and Sweet Tropical Raita

Most of us think of bananas only as sweet fruits that must be yellow and speckled with brown spots before they are ready to eat. In this recipe, we use unripe bananas for their wonderful texture and slight sweetness to create a sauce that is wonderful on top of brown basmati saffron rice, black beans, and other hearty, starchy dishes. If you have a hard time finding shredded unsweetened coconut, you might have to crack open a whole one. That's not an easy process, but the freshly harvested flesh is worth it.

Makes 5 cups

INGREDIENTS

- 3 large almost green bananas, peeled and sliced
- ½ cup shredded or cubed unsweetened coconut
- 2 cups plain yogurt (page 73)
- 1 small hot green chile, seeded and finely diced
- 1 tablespoon brown, black, or yellow mustard seeds, dry toasted and then coarsely ground
- 2–4 teaspoons fresh lemon juice
- 2–4 teaspoons extra-virgin olive oil
- Salt and freshly ground black pepper

STEPS

1. Combine the bananas and coconut in a medium bowl.

2. Stir in the yogurt, chile, mustard seeds, lemon juice, and oil. Season to taste with salt and pepper.

3. Cover and chill in the refrigerator for a few hours to improve the flavor. When you're ready to serve, stir, taste again, and season as needed. This raita will keep for about 1 week in the fridge.

Tzatziki

This Greek classic has been introduced to most Americans through the gyro sandwich. Homemade tsatziki is great on roast beef sandwiches, day-after-Thanksgiving turkey sandwiches, portobello burgers, and, of course, lamb and beef gyros! My first Greek recipes came from my mom's cookbook, published in 1950, called *Can the Greeks Cook!* It's still a great resource, and you can find used copies online.

Makes 3 cups

INGREDIENTS

- 2 cups drained plain yogurt (page 73), plain kefir (page 97 or 100), or yogurt or kefir sour cream (page 139)
- 1 medium cucumber, peeled, seeded, and finely minced
- 1 garlic clove, minced
- 2 teaspoons extra-virgin olive oil
- 2 teaspoons apple cider vinegar or fresh lemon juice
- ½ teaspoon salt

STEPS

Combine the yogurt, cucumber, garlic, oil, vinegar, and salt in a medium bowl. Mix well. Cover and refrigerate. It will keep for about 1 week in the refrigerator.

Creamy Baba Ghanoush

I was introduced to baba ghanoush by some wonderful foodie neighbors who lived near us in Washington, D.C. I already knew and loved hummus, but baba ghanoush, from Lebanon and Syria, is even creamier and more savory. Adding some drained yogurt or kefir adds another layer of flavor, tang, and richness.

There's nothing "light" about baba ghanoush — drizzles and swirls of olive oil are part of its charm and deliciousness. Feel free to adjust the seasoning amounts to your taste.

Makes 4–5 cups

INGREDIENTS

2–3 medium eggplants (1½–2 pounds total)

⅛–¼ cup extra-virgin olive oil, plus more for oiling the pan

1 cup drained plain yogurt (page 73) or drained plain kefir (page 97 or 100)

½ cup tahini

2 tablespoons fresh lemon juice

2 garlic cloves, minced or juiced

¼ teaspoon smoked or plain paprika

1 teaspoon za'atar (optional)

2 tablespoons chopped fresh cilantro or parsley

STEPS

1. Preheat the oven to 350°F (180°C). Oil a baking sheet, or for easier cleanup, line a baking sheet with parchment paper and then oil the paper.

2. Cut the eggplants in half lengthwise and place facedown on the oiled baking sheet. Roast for 1 hour, or until wilted. Remove from the oven and let cool.

3. Scoop the eggplant innards into the bowl of a food processor. Purée until smooth. Add ⅛ to ¼ cup oil, depending on how oily you like it, along with the yogurt, tahini, lemon juice, and garlic, and purée again.

4. Just before serving, sprinkle with paprika and za'atar, if using, and top with chopped cilantro. This baba ghanoush will keep for about 1 week in the refrigerator.

French Onion "Soup" Dip

Sure, you can make onion dip from scratch by sautéing fresh onions and shallots, but it will never taste like the guilty pleasure dip made from a packet of powdered French onion soup mix. I admit to being so desperate for that not-so-naturally flavored dip that I've grabbed whatever powdered and dried spice seemed like a good fit and mixed it in with some sour cream — usually not even waiting for the flavors to meld. When you want it, you want it! This recipe is a nice balance between the honest-to-goodness fresh onion version and the MSG-laced packet. In this recipe, miso's umami power creates the familiar savory flavor, but you can substitute soy or tamari sauce or even a bouillon cube. It's a very flexible recipe — as long as you have dried minced onions and a few other spices, you can likely make an onion dip that will satisfy everyone.

Makes 2 cups

INGREDIENTS

- 2 cups yogurt sour cream (page 139) or kefir crème fraîche (page 136)
- 2 tablespoons dried minced onions
- 2 teaspoons yellow miso paste
- 1 teaspoon onion or garlic powder
- 1 teaspoon dried parsley or 1 tablespoon finely chopped fresh parsley
- ¼ teaspoon salt
- ¼ teaspoon freshly cracked black pepper

STEPS

1. Combine the sour cream, dried onions, miso, onion powder, parsley, salt, and pepper in a large bowl and stir to blend well.

2. Cover and chill in the refrigerator for 1 to 2 hours to allow the flavors to marry and the dried spices to soften. This dip will keep for 1 to 2 weeks in the refrigerator.

Pakistani Lauki ka Raita (Bottle Gourd Dip)

The bottle gourd, also known as calabash, is often picked when young and used in Middle Eastern cooking as a fresh green squash. This recipe comes straight from Pakistan courtesy of the wife of my yogurt-making friend Mujtaba Safdar (profiled on page 169). You can find simpler Western versions of this recipe online, but none will duplicate the complexity and nuances of this one. This recipe calls for chaat masala — a wonderful Pakistani spice blend — and some fresh or dried curry leaves (no, these are not the same as curry powder). You can find these at many Asian markets, or online. If you can't find young bottle gourds, use chayote squash instead. If you can't find curry leaves, omit them — there is no good substitute.

Makes 2 cups

INGREDIENTS

- 1 cup mashed, steamed bottle gourd
- 1 cup drained plain yogurt (page 73)
- 4 garlic cloves, minced
- 1 teaspoon chaat masala
- Salt and freshly ground black pepper

- 2 tablespoons extra-virgin olive oil
- 1 fresh green chile, minced
- 2 curry leaves (also known as sweet neem)
- 1 teaspoon cumin seeds

STEPS

1. Combine the squash and yogurt in a medium bowl. Add one of the minced garlic cloves and the chaat masala and stir well. Season with salt and pepper to taste.

2. Heat the oil in a pan over medium heat. Add the chile and the remaining 3 cloves of minced garlic and sauté for about 2 minutes. Stir in the curry leaves and cumin seeds and cook briefly, about 10 seconds. Pour the oil mixture over the dip and serve.

Orban Creamery

RAWALPINDI, PAKISTAN

Mujtaba Safdar grew up where yogurt, known there as dahi, was born and nurtured into its present form. During his childhood in Rawalpindi, which is near Islamabad, Pakistan, Mujtaba developed a passion for animals as well as the knowledge of how to make dahi. His father kept the family's water buffalo at a nearby farm and brought the rich milk home, where it was made into fresh, traditional yogurt. "That love for yogurt and cheese greatly enriched my aspiration to have a dairy business of some sort when I first went to the United States and tasted different kinds of yogurt," Mujtaba says. "So, after almost a decade, I left the U.S. thinking about starting a business back home in Pakistan."

Even though yogurt has been made in his part of the world for thousands of years, Mujtaba was inspired by the flavor and texture of some of the yogurt he tasted in the United States — particularly drained, or Greek, yogurt. He set about his business with a desire to bring that style of yogurt to Pakistani consumers. But, as he says, "passion itself does not make one consistent. Consistency with patience is what is required to perfect one's craft."

Finding enough high-quality milk was the hardest part of the business, and it still is. When he first started his company, it took Mujtaba two years to find the right milk, and he is still struggling to find enough quality milk, while at the same time he is working to perfect his craft. "Market dynamics," he says, "are changing rapidly in my country." While an encouraging organic movement has engulfed the dairy industry, the demand for organic milk has driven up the cost. For Mujtaba, who makes a drained yogurt with up to half the yield of thinner yogurt, this results in a bottom-line price that is beyond what most customers are accustomed to.

Although Pakistan is still one of the world's major producers of water buffalo milk, second only to India, added costs have meant that cow dairies have now become more common. The cow's milk is less expensive, though still quite costly, but it does offer Mujtaba the opportunity to make cream-top yogurt — a unique product in the region. Another unique factor for his products is the addition of probiotic strains of bacteria and the absence of any added sugar, neither of which he says any of his competitors are doing. He plans on adding other varieties, including some flavored with the seasonings of traditional Pakistani dips such as lauki (bottle gourd) dip (page 168).

As is the case for other small producers around the world, challenges abound. You can follow Mujtaba's efforts and Orban Creamery (*orban* means "urban") on Facebook and Instagram.

Greek Goddess Dressing

The classic green goddess dressing lends itself beautifully to a yogurt revision. The original contains a variety of leafy green herbs, sour cream, and anchovies. For this recipe, I use drained yogurt instead of sour cream and miso and nutritional yeast instead of anchovies to make it vegetarian. Feel free to use anchovies, however, if you prefer. For a dip, drain the yogurt longer or use the yogurt fromage blanc recipe on page 131.

Makes about 1 cup

INGREDIENTS

- ½ cup drained plain yogurt (page 73) or plain kefir (page 97 or 100) (drain the yogurt or kefir to 50% to 75% of its original volume)
- ¼ cup mayonnaise
- ⅛ cup extra-virgin olive oil
- 1 cup loosely packed parsley leaves
- ¼ cup fresh tarragon or 1 tablespoon dried
- 3 tablespoons chopped fresh chives
- 1 teaspoon red or yellow miso paste
- 1 tablespoon nutritional yeast
- 1 tablespoon fresh lemon juice
- Salt and freshly ground black pepper

STEPS

Combine the yogurt, mayonnaise, oil, parsley, tarragon, chives, miso, nutritional yeast, lemon juice, and salt and pepper to taste in a food processor or blender and blend until smooth. If the dressing is too thick, add more lemon juice and oil to thin. The dressing can be used fresh, but it is better after being chilled in the refrigerator for a few hours. It will keep for 1 to 2 weeks in the refrigerator.

Really Ranch Dressing

Eaten as a dip with fries, pizza, fried chicken, and any number of other dishes — such as battered and pan-fried Quick 'n' Squeaky Curds (page 153), shown at right — ranch dressing is ubiquitous here in the States. I don't know how this happened, but it shows the flavor appeal of blending a dairy ferment (buttermilk) with herbs and spices. Here, I use yogurt or kefir in place of buttermilk. Many recipes use dried spices, but I like the flavor of fresh. Feel free to use either; both will give you that classic bottled-ranch flavor.

Makes 2 cups

INGREDIENTS

½ cup mayonnaise

½ cup yogurt sour cream (page 139)

½ cup plain yogurt (page 73) or plain kefir (page 97 or 100)

1 tablespoon fresh lemon juice

1 garlic clove, minced, or ¼ teaspoon garlic powder

2 tablespoons chopped onion or 1 teaspoon onion powder

1 tablespoon chopped fresh chives or 1 teaspoon dried

1 tablespoon chopped fresh dill or 1 teaspoon dried

1 tablespoon chopped fresh parsley or 1 teaspoon dried

½ teaspoon mustard powder

Salt and freshly ground black pepper

STEPS

Combine the mayonnaise, sour cream, yogurt, lemon juice, garlic, onion, chives, dill, parsley, mustard, and salt and pepper to taste in a food processor or blender and blend until smooth. If the dressing is too thick, add more lemon juice to thin. The dressing can be used fresh, but it is better after being chilled for a few hours. It will keep for 1 to 2 weeks in the refrigerator.

Curry Dip

When most Americans use the word *curry*, we are referring to the spice mixture that we associate with Indian food. As with many dishes that Westerners think of as ethnic, however, curry powder is definitely not Indian, but rather a British invention, albeit inspired by the cuisine of India. It is, no matter its provenance, definitely wonderful! For a milder version, omit the cayenne pepper. I find that curry blends bring out sweetness in foods, so I prefer mine with quite a bit of hot pepper.

Makes 2 cups

INGREDIENTS

- 2 cups yogurt sour cream (page 139) or kefir crème fraîche (page 136)
- 1 garlic clove, minced or juiced, or ¼ teaspoon garlic powder
- 2 teaspoons curry powder
- 2 teaspoons fresh lemon juice
- ½ teaspoon ground coriander
- ½ teaspoon salt
- ½ teaspoon ground turmeric
- ¼ teaspoon ground cayenne pepper
- ¼ cup chopped cilantro, for garnish

STEPS

Combine the sour cream, garlic, curry powder, lemon juice, coriander, salt, turmeric, and cayenne in a medium bowl and mix well. Taste, and add more salt or cayenne, if you like. Just before serving, top with cilantro. This dip can be made ahead and refrigerated for up to 1 week.

Creamy Garlic Balsamic Dressing

My favorite dressing is always simple olive oil and vinegar. Growing up, I had never heard of balsamic vinegar, but thankfully it's now easy to find — albeit not always of the best quality. In this recipe I replace a bit of the oil with yogurt for a dramatically different result. You can add nutritional yeast, one of my favorite salad ingredients, for thickness, umami, and nutritional benefit.

Makes 1 cup

INGREDIENTS

½ cup extra-virgin olive oil

¼ cup balsamic vinegar, or to taste

¼ cup plain yogurt (page 73), drained for a thicker dressing or undrained for a thinner one

1 garlic clove, juiced or minced

¼ teaspoon freshly ground black pepper

1 tablespoon nutritional yeast (optional)

STEPS

Combine the oil, vinegar, yogurt, garlic, pepper, and nutritional yeast, if using, in a medium bowl and whisk well. Use fresh or chilled. The dressing will keep for 1 to 2 weeks in the refrigerator.

Chilled and Creamy Soups

A dollop of yogurt or a drizzle of kefir makes almost any steaming bowl of soup better. The recipes in this chapter take dairy ferments from the sidelines to the center of attention — and keep their probiotics lively and viable. Kefir usually adds a bit more acid than yogurt, and you can always adjust the sourness level by adding vinegar or lemon juice. If you use a drained yogurt, you might need to add liquid such as broth, whey, or water to thin it to a soupier texture. I hope it goes without saying that you should choose plain, unsweetened dairy ferments for these recipes.

Roasted Chioggia Beet Chlodnik

Most recipes for chlodnik (cold Polish beet soup) use dark beets that have been either fermented or simmered, along with beet greens, to create a deep ruby-red mixture. For this recipe, I used mild and beautiful Italian heirloom Chioggia beets. Instead of boiling the beets, I roast and then cube them. The resulting soup has a milder, sweeter flavor than its traditional counterpart. Try it both ways!

Makes 7–8 cups

INGREDIENTS

3–4 Chioggia beets, roasted, peeled, and coarsely chopped

2 quarts plain kefir (page 97 or 100)

1 large cucumber, peeled, seeded, and finely chopped

1 bunch radishes, thinly sliced

¼ cup fresh lemon juice, or to taste

2 tablespoons chopped fresh dill, plus extra for garnish

Salt and freshly ground black pepper

1 hard-boiled egg, quartered or sliced (optional)

Sliced sausage, such as kielbasa (optional)

Hot sauce (optional)

STEPS

1. Place the beets in a food processor and purée until smooth. Slowly add 1 quart of the kefir and continue to blend until smooth. Pour the purée into a large bowl, add the remaining 1 quart kefir, and stir to blend.

2. Stir in the cucumber and radishes. Add the lemon juice, using more or less as desired to create whatever level of tanginess you prefer.

3. Add the dill, and season to taste with salt and pepper. Chill for at least 3 hours and up to overnight. Serve garnished with fresh dill, and egg, sausage, and hot sauce, if desired. This soup will keep for about 1 week in the refrigerator.

Cool Corn Chowder

Chowder doesn't need to be confined to the winter months. On a hot summer day or during a late-fall heat wave, this cool chowder is both hearty and comforting. I made this recipe vegetarian, but you can easily include clams if you like. When I was developing this recipe, my tasters all agreed that when left in cubes, the potatoes seemed out of place. When puréed, however, they add creaminess and body.

Makes 5–8 cups

INGREDIENTS

- 2 medium potatoes, diced (I don't peel them, just scrub well first)
- ¼ cup dried shiitake mushrooms
- 4 tablespoons extra-virgin olive oil
- 1 teaspoon toasted sesame oil
- 1 cup sliced fresh white button or crimini mushrooms
- 2 stalks celery, chopped
- ½ sweet onion, minced
- ¼ teaspoon fresh or dried thyme leaves
- ½ cup milk, white wine, or broth or stock of choice, plus more as needed
- Kernels sliced from 2 ears fresh corn (see note)
- 1 tablespoon fresh lemon juice
- 1 teaspoon tamari or soy sauce
- 2 cups plain yogurt (page 73)
- Salt and freshly ground black pepper

STEPS

1. Place the potatoes in a saucepan with enough water to cover. Set over medium-high heat and boil until tender but not falling apart, 5 to 8 minutes depending on potato type. Drain, reserving 1 cup of the liquid. Purée the potatoes in a food processor or mash by hand. Set aside to cool.

2. Place the shiitakes in a medium bowl and pour the reserved hot potato water over them. Place a small bowl on top of the mushrooms to keep them submerged. Soak until rehydrated, 10 to 30 minutes.

3. Heat the olive oil and sesame oil in a skillet over medium heat. Add the button mushrooms, celery, onion, and thyme, and sauté until tender but not mushy, 5 to 8 minutes. Place the vegetables in a large bowl.

4. Return the skillet to the heat and pour in the wine to deglaze the pan. Pour the wine and any bits you were able to scrape up from the pan over the sautéed vegetables.

5. Drain the shiitake mushroom liquid into the vegetable mixture. Chop the shiitakes and stir them into the vegetable mix.

6. Add the corn, lemon juice, tamari, and cooled potatoes, then stir in the yogurt. Add more milk to thin to your desired consistency, then season with salt and pepper to taste. Chill in the refrigerator for at least 3 hours before serving. This chowder will keep for about 1 week in the refrigerator.

NOTE: *If you can make this soup at the peak of summer with fresh corn on the cob picked that same day, then leave it raw — it's delicious! Otherwise, give the corn a quick cook by steaming in the microwave while still wrapped in husks or in hot water. Don't overcook; usually a couple of minutes will do.*

Persian Fusion Yogurt Soup

Classic Persian *ab doogh khiar* (yogurt cucumber soup) utilizes some of the same classic flavors you find in other yogurt soups, including cucumbers and dill. Some recipes include other herbs, such as tarragon and savory. Raisins and walnuts add sweetness and crunch, and bits of dried flatbread are mixed in at the last moment. For this recipe, I added other spices and herbs as well as coconut milk. The result is delicious and slightly exotic, and it pairs well with Indian as well as Persian dishes.

Makes 7–8 cups

INGREDIENTS

- 4 medium cucumbers, peeled and coarsely chopped
- 2 shallots, coarsely chopped
- 1–2 garlic cloves, minced
- ¼ cup extra-virgin olive oil
- 4 cups plain yogurt (page 73)
- 1 (15-ounce) can coconut milk
- ¼ cup fresh lemon juice
- ½ cup golden raisins
- ¼ cup chopped fresh cilantro
- 1 (1-inch) piece ginger, grated
- 2 tablespoons chopped fresh mint
- 1 teaspoon tamarind paste
- ¼ teaspoon ground coriander
- Salt and freshly ground black pepper
- ½ cup chopped walnuts
- Rose petals, for garnish

STEPS

1. Combine the cucumbers, shallots, and garlic in a food processor and purée. Slowly add the oil and purée until smooth. Pour into a mixing bowl.

2. Add the yogurt, coconut milk, and lemon juice, and stir until well combined.

3. Add the raisins, cilantro, ginger, mint, tamarind paste, and coriander, and stir until evenly blended. Season with salt and pepper to taste. Chill in the refrigerator for at least 4 hours and up to overnight. When you serve the soup, top individual bowls with chopped walnuts and garnish with rose petals. The soup will keep for about 1 week in the refrigerator.

Gazpacho Blanco

I first tasted this amazing Spanish classic more than 20 years ago at the incredible tapas restaurant Jaleo in Washington, D.C. We were on our way to see a Shakespeare play at the historic Folger Theatre, and I can't remember what play we saw but I never forgot the soup! I found a copy of the recipe, and I've been making it ever since.

Bread is a main ingredient in most traditional gazpachos, but I find that yogurt easily adds a similar body and mouthfeel. Of all of the gazpachos I have tried, this one is the most unique, surprising, and satisfying. It's hearty enough to be a main course for a dinner party and refreshing and enticing enough to serve in a tiny cup as an *amuse-bouche* before almost any meal. I've even served it at Thanksgiving to great accolades.

Makes 5–7 cups

INGREDIENTS

- ⅔ cup slivered almonds
- 2 garlic cloves
- 1 teaspoon salt
- ½ green melon, such as honeydew, diced
- 6 tablespoons extra-virgin olive oil

- 1 tablespoon sherry vinegar
- 2 tablespoons apple cider vinegar
- 2 cups plain yogurt (page 73)
- 1 cup ice cubes and water
- Green seedless grapes or melon balls, for garnish

STEPS

1. Combine the almonds, garlic, and salt in a food processor or blender and process until fine, about 1 minute.

2. Add the melon, oil, sherry vinegar, apple cider vinegar, and yogurt, and process until smooth and creamy, about 2 minutes.

3. Fill a 1-cup measuring cup with ice cubes. Add water to fill the cup. Add the ice and water to the gazpacho and purée until the ice is dissolved or crushed fine, about 1 minute. Serve cold. Just before serving, add 6 to 8 grapes per serving. If the grapes are large, cut them in half. The gazpacho will keep for about 1 week in the refrigerator.

Gazpacho Rosado

I adapted this recipe from the classic tomato gazpacho. Thanks to the inclusion of yogurt, the brilliant red of the original is tinted a pretty pink, or *rosado*. Gazpacho rosado is not only teeming with probiotics, but it is also a great source of the carotenoid lycopene, a powerful antioxidant. The olive oil in the soup helps your body absorb the fat-soluble lycopene, and it also rounds out the mouthfeel and balances the acidity. Gazpacho rosado makes a great main course on a hot summer day, a drinkable salad, or a palate cleanser between heavier courses. Do try to locate a bottle of sherry vinegar; it's worth the effort to add an authentic Spanish nuance. The recipe is best made at the peak of summer when all of the veggies are fresh, but canned stewed tomatoes can be substituted if you're craving the dish off-season.

Makes 6–8 cups

INGREDIENTS

- 2 pounds fresh tomatoes
- 1 small sweet yellow onion, such as Vidalia or Walla Walla, one half chopped and the other half finely chopped
- 1 large cucumber, peeled, one half sliced and the other half finely chopped
- 1 hot pepper, such as jalapeño, seeded, one half roughly chopped and the other half finely chopped (optional)

- 2 yellow bell peppers, one half roughly chopped and the other half finely chopped
- 1 garlic clove
- 4 fresh basil leaves, two left whole and two thinly sliced
- 2 cups plain yogurt (page 73)
- ¼ cup extra-virgin olive oil
- 2 tablespoons sherry vinegar (or red wine or balsamic vinegar in a pinch)
- Salt and freshly ground black pepper

STEPS

1. Core the tomatoes. If they are small or heavy-skinned, blanch them briefly in boiling water and then remove their skins. Purée in a food processor or with an immersion blender until smooth.

2. Add the chopped onion to the tomato mixture. Place the finely chopped onion in a separate medium bowl.

3. Add the sliced cucumber to the tomato mixture. Add the finely chopped cucumber to the onion bowl.

4. Add the roughly chopped hot pepper and bell pepper to the tomato mixture. Add the finely chopped hot pepper and bell pepper to the onion mixture.

5. Add the garlic to the tomato mixture.

6. Add the whole basil leaves to the tomato mixture. Set aside the thinly sliced basil leaves.

7. Purée the tomato mixture until smooth. Add the yogurt, oil, and vinegar to the tomato mixture and purée until well blended. Season to taste with salt and black pepper.

8. Stir in most of the chopped veggies; they will add a lovely texture. Just before serving, sprinkle the top of the soup with the remaining chopped veggies and the sliced basil leaves. You can also drizzle the soup with a bit more oil and place a dollop of yogurt at the center of the bowl (before sprinkling on the chopped veggies) for effect. This gazpacho will keep for about 1 week in the refrigerator.

Borscht and Kin

In eastern Europe and Russia, tangy, ferment-based soups, including Russian borscht and Polish chlodnik (see the recipe on page 177), are not only traditional but quite popular. The sour base is often created by the natural lactofermentation of beet greens and roots, cucumbers, or other vegetables. These fermented vegetables are then combined with myriad chopped herbs, fresh vegetables, and broth. Most varieties are also served with sausages and chopped hard-boiled eggs, creating a tasty, balanced, nutritious meal. Although traditional borscht is served warm, chilled versions are popular in the summer in many Baltic and eastern European countries, including Lithuania and the Ukraine. Cold versions often include a dairy ferment either as the liquid base or as a topping.

As with most traditional dishes, once you know the basics, you can let your own taste buds and what's in your fridge and garden dictate the ingredients. Simply strive for a balance of sweet and sour (provided by yogurt, kefir, lemon juice, fresh veggies, and maybe even a touch of sugar), texture and flavor (provided by chopped veggies and herbs), and protein (from hard-boiled eggs and/or sausages). Simple and delicious!

Okroshka with Watermelon Radish, New Potatoes, and Beer

A Russian and Ukrainian classic, okroshka traditionally relies upon dark, tangy fermented kvass as its base. This recipe instead utilizes the acidic qualities of yogurt and German-style lager beer. For a nonalcoholic version, you can substitute sparkling water for the beer. There is great similarity, as you can see from the ingredients, between okroshka and chlodnik (page 177).

Makes 7–8 cups

INGREDIENTS

- 4 cups plain yogurt (page 73)
- 1 cup finely chopped mint, plus a few mint leaves for garnish
- 1 cup finely chopped parsley
- ¼ cup apple cider vinegar
- 1–2 tablespoons freshly grated or prepared horseradish
- 2 English cucumbers, peeled and seeded, one finely chopped and the other thinly sliced

- 1 bunch watermelon radishes (or combination of regular and watermelon varieties), half finely chopped and half sliced
- Salt and freshly ground black pepper
- 2 cups diced, cooked new potatoes
- 1–2 (12-ounce) bottles lager or other ale, or 1½–3 cups sparkling water
- Shredded or chopped ham, for a more traditional, heartier meal (optional)

STEPS

1. Pour the yogurt into a large bowl and add the mint, parsley, vinegar, and horseradish. Whisk to combine.

2. Stir in the cucumbers and radishes, then season to taste with salt and pepper. Stir in the potatoes. Refrigerate for at least 4 hours and up to overnight.

3. Just before serving, stir in the beer. Garnish with whole mint leaves and ham, if desired. The soup will keep for about 1 week in the refrigerator.

Beverages and Libations

Yogurt and kefir are made for sipping! Their tang and smooth texture make them a natural fit for an unlimited number of beverages. In this chapter I've included classic Indian lassis, very American smoothies, and some unforgettable cocktails. Hopefully you'll be inspired by these examples and discover how easy it is to adapt ingredients on hand to craft some satisfying sippers.

Whey Berry 'n' Ginger Punch

If you make Greek yogurt (page 56), you're going to have a decent amount of whey left over, and here's one way to use it. The lactose in the whey gives this punch recipe a much more pleasing mouthfeel than most fruity drinks. If you want to increase the volume but don't have a lot of whey, you can add some pineapple juice or even some yogurt.

Makes 5 cups

INGREDIENTS

2 cups yogurt whey

1 cup fresh berries

1 cup pineapple juice

1 tablespoon freshly grated ginger

1 cup sparkling cider or soda water (for more or less sweetness)

Simple syrup (page 213), honey syrup (equal parts hot water and honey), or sugar (optional)

STEPS

1. Combine the whey and berries in a medium bowl. Muddle the fruit.

2. Add the pineapple juice and ginger, and stir to combine. Stir in the sparkling cider and sweetener, if using. Chill in the refrigerator before serving.

Lassi

Lassi (pronounced *luu-see*) is an Indian beverage made of lightly seasoned yogurt thinned with water. It can be salty or sweet, and its flavor is very much dependent on the quality of the yogurt. Unlike American-style smoothies, lassis are meant to be thin and refreshing.

You can find rose water at Indian and some Asian markets, as well as online. It's worth buying and is delicious in other recipes, including frozen yogurt, panna cotta, pastries, and more. For a truly "special" lassi, see the box on page 190.

Makes 2 cups

Simple Salty Lassi

- 1½ cups plain yogurt (page 73)
- ½ cup cold water (or water and ice cubes)
- ¼ teaspoon salt

Namkeen (Salty & Spicy) Lassi

- 1½ cups plain yogurt (page 73)
- ½ cup cold water (or water and ice cubes)
- ⅛–¼ teaspoon freshly toasted cumin seeds, lightly crushed
  - Salt (Indian black salt, or *kala namak*, is the best)
  - Black pepper (optional)
- 1–2 teaspoons chopped mint or cilantro

Classic Mango Lassi

- 1½ cups plain yogurt (page 73)
- ½ cup cold water (or water and ice cubes)
- ½–1 cup chopped ripe mango
- 2 tablespoons sugar or honey (omit if the mango is really sweet)

Rosewater and Cardamom Lassi

- 1½ cups plain yogurt (page 73)
- ½ cup cold water (or water and ice cubes)
- ⅛ cup sugar
- 2 teaspoons rose water
- ½ teaspoon ground cardamom
  - Pinch of dried or fresh rose petals (optional)

STEPS

Combine all of the ingredients in a blender and blend well. Serve over ice or straight up in a chilled glass. If you are so inclined, all of these recipes (with the exception of the bhang lassi; see the box on page 190) can be converted to cocktails with the addition of a shot or two of vodka.

Doogh

Persian doogh, or abdoogh, is about as simple a pleasure as you can find. A light and refreshing beverage, it is simply fresh yogurt thinned with icy cold water or soda water and lightly flavored with mint. Although almost identical to Indian lassis, doogh is defined by the use of mint.

Makes 3 cups

INGREDIENTS

2 cups plain yogurt (page 73)

⅛ teaspoon salt

1 teaspoon dried crushed mint leaves or 4 fresh mint leaves, plus mint sprigs for garnish

½–1 cup ice-cold water, sparkling or still

STEPS

1. Combine the yogurt, salt, and mint in a medium bowl. If you are using fresh mint leaves, crush, bruise, and/or chop them first.

2. Whisk in enough cold water to thin the mixture to the desired consistency. Serve in tall, chilled glasses, over ice, if desired. Garnish each with a mint sprig.

Weed Milkshake?

Yup. Bhang (cannabis) lassi is an iconic edible from India. As you might imagine, it has quite the following among tourists to India, where it can be purchased at government-authorized bhang shops. Bhang lassis have long been used in Hindu ceremonies and religious celebrations (not unlike how Native Americans used tobacco). To make it, blend small balls of cannabis paste (a few for a light version and many more for the acclimated or perhaps reckless) with yogurt, salt, water, and other spices, if desired. If you happen to be in India, or for that matter one of the growing number of U.S. states where recreational cannabis is legal, go easy on the bhang balls and time your experience for a period of reflection and contemplation — not right before an elephant ride!

Phoebe's Formula for a Green Smoothie

Our oldest daughter, Phoebe, loves smoothies. She has burned through a few bullet-style blenders and is now putting a new Vitamix to the test. Here's Phoebe's formula for a delicious, fiber- and nutrient-dense yogurt smoothie. If you want to play around with the recipe, she recommends shooting for 70 percent veggies to 30 percent fruit. She doesn't add any sweetener, counting instead on the natural sugars in the fruits to add sweetness. You can easily use yogurt whey or milk to thin the smoothie if it is too thick to suck through a straw!

Makes 4–6 cups

INGREDIENTS

2 bunches greens, such as kale, spinach, and/or lettuce

1–2 bananas

1–2 lemons

1 apple or pear

Handful of parsley

½ cup plain yogurt (page 73) or plain kefir (page 97 or 100)

¼ cup chia seeds, soaked overnight and then drained (optional)

1 tablespoon bee pollen (optional)

STEPS

Combine the greens, bananas, lemons, apple, parsley, yogurt, and chia seeds and bee pollen, if using, in a food processor or blender and purée until smooth. You may need to chop the greens, parsley, and apple first if you don't have a large-capacity unit. If you want to chill it, add ice cubes. Freeze any extra for enjoying later. The smoothie blend will keep for weeks if frozen.

Berry Good Smoothie

This smoothie is definitely more of a treat than the green version (page 191), but it's chock-full of antioxidants and is a wonderful midday snack on a hot summer afternoon.

Makes 3–4 cups

INGREDIENTS

- 1 cup fresh or frozen berries (any kind)
- 1 cup plain yogurt (page 73)
- 1 tablespoon honey, maple syrup, agave nectar, or other sweetener
- 1 teaspoon grated orange zest
- ¼ teaspoon vanilla extract

- 4–5 dates (optional)
- 1 banana (optional)
- 1 tablespoon rolled oats (optional)
- 1 teaspoon bee pollen (optional)
- ¼ teaspoon ground cinnamon or nutmeg (optional)

STEPS

Combine the berries, yogurt, honey, orange zest, vanilla, and dates, banana, oats, bee pollen, and cinnamon, if using, in a food processor or blender and purée until smooth. If you want to chill it, add ice cubes. Freeze any extra to help preserve the antioxidants. The smoothie blend will keep for weeks if frozen.

Limoncello Lift

We had the good fortune to visit Rome, Italy, a few years ago. Limoncello is ubiquitous there — conspicuously and unabashedly displayed to encourage tourists to take home one of the tall, attractive bottles. And, of course, we did. Once home, however, I wasn't sure what to do with it! This recipe came about in the hope of using up the souvenir. (So far, it's working.) Serve in a chilled martini glass for the prettiest presentation.

Makes 1 serving

INGREDIENTS

2 mint leaves

1 ounce white rum

1 tablespoon plain kefir (page 97 or 100) or plain yogurt (page 73)

1 tablespoon limoncello

¼ teaspoon grated lemon zest

Raw sugar, for the rim

1 lemon wedge, for the rim

Lemon peel twist, for garnish

STEPS

1. Muddle 1 mint leaf at the bottom of a cocktail shaker. Add the rum, kefir, limoncello, and lemon zest. Fill the shaker with ice and shake well.

2. Spread the raw sugar on a plate. Run a lemon wedge around the rim of a martini glass to moisten it, and dip the rim in the sugar to coat it. Pour the contents of the shaker into the glass (with or without ice cubes, as desired). Garnish with a lemon peel twist and remaining mint leaf. You can strain out the mint leaves or leave in.

Napitok Bogov

This drink is stunning, both in looks and in taste, and comes from James Beard Award–winning chef (and friend) Vitaly Paley of Paley's Place Bistro and Bar in Portland, Oregon. Paley, originally from the Ukraine, says the drink's name means "drink of the gods." Paley's Place bartender Jon Lawson gave it the name when he learned that kefir and honey have both been called food of the gods for thousands of years.

Makes 1 serving

INGREDIENTS

- 1¾ ounces Bombay Sapphire gin
- 1 ounce plain yogurt (page 73) or plain kefir (page 97 or 100)
- ½ ounce honey syrup (mix equal parts hot water and honey)
- ½ ounce fresh lemon juice
- ½ ounce fresh lime juice
- ¼ ounce cassis liquor or crème de cassis
- 1 egg white
- Dash of bitters (optional)
- Honeycomb, for garnish (optional)

STEPS

Combine the gin, yogurt, honey syrup, lemon juice, lime juice, cassis, egg white, and bitters, if using, in a cocktail shaker and shake well. Fill a glass with ice and pour the gin mixture over the ice. Top with a piece of honeycomb, if desired.

YoGimlet

This is probably my favorite gimlet, but I love a good gimlet of any kind! Try it both ways — with gin or with vodka. The difference is quite noticeable.

Makes 1 serving

INGREDIENTS

2 basil leaves

2 tablespoons sugar

¼ cucumber, peeled, seeded, and chopped, plus 1 thin slice of cucumber with peel

¼ cup fresh lime juice

1½ ounces gin or vodka

2 tablespoons plain yogurt (page 73)

STEPS

1. Muddle 1 basil leaf and the sugar in a cocktail shaker. Add the cucumber, lime juice, gin, and yogurt. Cover and chill in the refrigerator for at least 2 hours and up to overnight.

2. Place the cucumber slice in the bottom of a chilled glass. Add two ice cubes to the shaker, shake well, and pour into the glass (with or without the ice cubes, as desired). Garnish with the remaining basil leaf.

Whey 'n' Berry Mimosa

Mimosas are a brunch classic, but I always find them a little boring. In this recipe, yogurt whey adds silkiness to each sip, and the berries and mint bring out the best in the orange juice and sparkling wine. Remember this recipe when you are draining your next batch of yogurt!

Makes 1 serving

INGREDIENTS

2 mint leaves

2 strawberries, 4 raspberries, or a combination

4 ounces fresh or bottled orange juice

4 ounces yogurt whey

4–6 ounces prosecco, champagne, or sparkling cider

STEPS

Muddle 1 mint leaf and the berries in a glass. Add a few ice cubes, then pour in the orange juice and whey. Stir, then top off the glass with prosecco. You can make the base ahead of time, chill, and then add the bubbly when you're ready to serve.

Yogurita

The first time I experimented with making a margarita using yogurt, I was almost hoping it wouldn't turn out so that I would have to "test" the recipe more than once, but it was spot on. Tequila and yogurt make a surprisingly wonderful blend.

Makes 1 serving

INGREDIENTS

2 ounces silver tequila

½ ounce Cointreau

1 tablespoon fresh lime juice

1 tablespoon fresh orange juice

1 tablespoon plain yogurt (page 73)

¼ teaspoon grated orange zest

Citric acid powder, for the rim (optional)

Sugar, for the rim (optional)

Orange peel twist, for garnish

STEPS

1. Combine the tequila, Cointreau, lime juice, orange juice, yogurt, and orange zest in a cocktail shaker. Fill the shaker with ice and shake well.

2. If you would like to coat the rim of your glass with a sweet and sour mix, combine equal amounts of citric acid and sugar and spread on a plate. Moisten the rim of the glass with a bit of tequila, then dip the glass in the mixture of citric acid and sugar. Pour the contents of the shaker into the glass, with as much ice as desired, and garnish with an orange peel twist.

Kefir 'n' Cassis Sour

This is my take on the classic whiskey sour. Feel free to play around with the balance of sweet to sour. If the kefir isn't tart enough, or you want to use yogurt, add a bit of fresh lemon juice.

Makes 1 serving

INGREDIENTS

2 ounces bourbon

2 tablespoons plain kefir (page 97 or 100) or plain yogurt (page 73)

½ ounce crème de cassis

½ ounce simple syrup (page 213), or to taste

1 dash Angostura bitters

1 bourbon-soaked cocktail cherry (such as Jack Rudy brand), for garnish

STEPS

Combine the bourbon, kefir, crème de cassis, simple syrup, and bitters in a cocktail shaker and shake well. Serve on the rocks, garnished with a cherry.

Sweets and Treats

I saved the best for last — at least the best in overcoming our willpower! These delicious dessert recipes have the added benefit of probiotics, and fortunately not at the cost of any decadent experience. So have some fun, and enjoy the benefits and boundless potential of dairy ferments and take pleasure in a well-deserved indulgence!

French Custard-Style Frozen Yogurt

To retain a creamy texture, ice cream and frozen yogurt must include ingredients that limit the growth of ice crystals. The fat and moisture content of the yogurt as well as the form of the added sugar (see the tip on page 204) have a great influence on this. The greater the fat and the less the moisture, the richer and creamier the texture. French or custard-style recipes use egg yolks to achieve that creamy consistency — even as many as a dozen yolks per quart! The eggs add fat, but they also serve as an emulsifier, keeping ice crystals from growing too large. I'm not a fan of a really eggy taste, so I settled on six yolks for this recipe. You can experiment, using more or fewer yolks to suit your taste. You will need an ice cream maker to make this recipe.

Makes just over 1 quart

INGREDIENTS

2 cups heavy cream

¾ cup sugar

6 egg yolks

⅛ teaspoon salt

1½ cups plain yogurt (page 73)

1 tablespoon vanilla extract

STEPS

1. Combine 1 cup of the heavy cream and the sugar in small saucepan over medium heat. Heat, stirring constantly, until just about simmering, about 8 minutes. Remove from the heat.

2. Whisk together the egg yolks and salt in a medium bowl. While whisking the eggs, add a small amount of the hot cream to the yolks. Slowly add the rest of the hot cream in a steady stream, whisking constantly, until it is incorporated.

3. Pour the egg mixture into the warm saucepan you used to heat the cream and set it over medium-low heat. Cook, stirring constantly, until the mixture thickens slightly, about 2 minutes. If you are checking the temperature, it will be about 170°F (77°C). Don't allow it to boil.

Recipe continues on next page

French Custard-Style Frozen Yogurt *continued*

4. Place a sieve over a bowl. Strain the mixture through the sieve, then chill, uncovered or lightly covered with plastic wrap or a cloth, in the refrigerator for at least 1 hour.

5. When the custard base is chilled, add the yogurt and vanilla. Blend, using an immersion blender or whisk, until smooth. Cover the bowl and chill in a very cold refrigerator for about 8 hours, or in the freezer for about 4 hours. If you are chilling in a freezer, stir the mixture every 15 minutes or so. You don't want it to freeze, just to get very cold.

6. Prepare your ice cream maker as directed by the manufacturer and churn the mix.

7. If you like your yogurt soft, you can enjoy it right away. If you want a firmer frozen yogurt, harden it for a few hours in the freezer. It's a good idea to prechill the hardening container so that the frozen yogurt doesn't melt when you place it in the container. Turn the frozen yogurt into the chilled container, pack smooth, cover, and place in a deep freezer or the coldest part of your freezer.

8. The best serving temperature for ice cream and frozen yogurt is 0°F (−18°C), which is the normal temperature for most home freezers. If you've hardened yours in a deep freezer, which is much colder, move it to the freezer compartment of your refrigerator for an hour or so before serving. Alternatively, you can set the container in the fridge for a bit, but don't forget it, or you'll be back to the milkshake stage.

Simplest Frozen Yogurt

Making any frozen yogurt or ice cream recipe at home takes a bit of planning to make sure that all your equipment and ingredients are at their coldest — unless a milkshake consistency is your goal. Compared to the custard-base recipe on page 201, this recipe requires much less preparation and is ready to churn more quickly. Because it lacks egg yolks, you can expect a firmer texture after the hardening stage. It can be softened by using honey or simple syrup instead of granulated sugar. I adore the flavor that honey provides — especially in its balancing effect on tangy yogurt — but it is optional. This basic recipe can be tweaked in so many directions, depending on what you have on hand and your own preferences. The sky's the limit! Here are three versions, in increasing level of richness, to get you primed.

Makes about 1 quart

Greek 'n' Honey Frozen Yogurt

    3 cups drained plain yogurt
       (page 73)
  1½ tablespoons vanilla extract
   ½ cup honey or simple syrup
       (page 213), or a combination
       Pinch of salt

Cream 'n' Greek Frozen Yogurt

  1½ cups drained plain yogurt
       (page 73)
  1½ cups yogurt sour cream (page 139)
       or unwhipped yogurt crème fraîche
       (page 136)
   ½ cup honey or simple syrup
       (page 213) or a combination
  1½ tablespoons vanilla extract
       Pinch of salt

Fromage Blanc 'n' Cream Frozen Yogurt

    1 cup yogurt fromage blanc
       (page 131)
    2 cups heavy cream
   ½ cup honey or simple syrup
       (page 213), or a combination
  1½ tablespoons vanilla extract
       Pinch of salt (unless the yogurt
       cheese is salted)

STEPS

1. Combine all the ingredients in a medium bowl and mix thoroughly with an immersion blender or whisk. Cover the bowl and chill in a very cold refrigerator or in the freezer. If you are chilling in a freezer, stir the mixture every 15 minutes or so. You don't want it to freeze, just to get very cold.

Recipe continues on next page

2. Prepare your ice cream churn as directed by the manufacturer and churn the mix.

3. If you like your yogurt soft, you can enjoy it right away. If you want a firmer frozen yogurt, harden it for a few hours in the freezer. It's a good idea to prechill the hardening container so that the frozen yogurt doesn't melt when you place it in the container. Turn the frozen yogurt into the chilled container, pack smooth, cover, and place in a deep freezer or the coldest part of your freezer.

4. The best serving temperature for ice cream and frozen yogurt is 0°F (−18°C), which is the normal temperature for most home freezers. If you've hardened yours in a deep freezer, which is much colder, move it to the freezer compartment of your refrigerator for an hour or so before serving. Alternatively, you can set the container in the fridge for a bit, but don't forget it, or you'll be back to the milkshake stage.

Sweet Science of Silky Ice Cream

In chapter 2, you learned that the star of milk fermentation is the sugar molecule lactose. If you recall, lactose is composed of two simple sugars, glucose and galactose, making it a disaccharide. Table sugar (sucrose) is also a disaccharide — it is the joined sugars glucose and fructose. When glucose and fructose join together, they take on a crystallized form. Although crystallized sugar is great when you are baking cookies and rimming your cocktail glass, it's not so great when you want to dissolve sugar in your iced tea or make creamy frozen desserts. Not only is it hard to dissolve, but it also contributes to the hardness of the ice cream, making it difficult to scoop.

When glucose and fructose are separated, however, and added to frozen dairy products in a liquid state, they create a softness that allows for easier scooping and a much more pleasing texture. They do this by lowering the freezing point of the product. For example, if you made two batches of frozen yogurt, one with granulated sugar and one with honey, which is made of glucose and fructose as separate sugars (monosaccharides), the sugar batch would be super hard when it came out of the freezer and the honey batch would be softer.

Because of this fact, I use real corn syrup (also known as glucose syrup and not to be confused with high-fructose corn syrup) in some recipes, as well as agave nectar (high in fructose), honey (glucose and fructose), and simple syrup (glucose and fructose).

Yogurt-Cheese Pie

When I was a kid, my mom used to make a cream cheese pie that was to die for, or at least I thought so at the time. It included sweetened condensed milk, had a graham cracker crust, and was always topped by glistening canned cherry pie filling. I shudder now when I consider the total amount of sugar in the original recipe! For my adaptation, you'll need to drain plain yogurt to the thickest consistency possible — making what is often called yogurt cheese — or use well-drained yogurt/kefir fromage blanc. My recipe does use sweetened condensed milk, but half the original volume. A quick sprinkle of granola forms the crust, and lightly sweetened canned tart cherries form the topping. You can make it as a pie or in individual cups; I like to use small glass cups so that the layers are visible. If you find that this recipe isn't as sweet as you would like it, you can double the amount of sugar in the cherry topping or use a sweeter granola.

Makes one 9-inch pie

INGREDIENTS

- 1 cup fully drained plain yogurt (page 73) or yogurt or kefir fromage blanc (page 131)
- ½ cup sweetened condensed milk
- 1 tablespoon fresh lemon juice
- 1 teaspoon grated lemon zest

- ½ cup plain or cinnamon granola, with or without nuts, for the crust (or use any graham cracker–type crust)
- 1 (15-ounce) can unsweetened tart cherries
- 2 tablespoons sugar
- 1 tablespoon cornstarch

STEPS

1. Combine the yogurt, sweetened condensed milk, and lemon juice and zest in a medium bowl. Using an immersion blender or whisk, blend until smooth and creamy.

2. Sprinkle the granola on the bottom of a 9-inch pie pan, four ramekins, or small glasses. Add the creamy filling, cover, and chill in the refrigerator to set, 4 to 6 hours for individual servings or 8 to 10 hours for a small pie.

3. Drain the liquid from the canned cherries into a small bowl. Pour the cherries into a small saucepan and stir in the sugar.

4. Add the cornstarch to the reserved cherry liquid and stir until well combined.

5. Add the cornstarch mix to the cherries in the pan and set over medium-low heat. Cook, stirring constantly, until the mixture begins to bubble. Cook gently for 1 minute longer, then remove from the heat, let cool, and chill and store in the refrigerator.

6. When the cherry mixture is cold and the pies are set, top the pies with the cherry mixture and serve.

Chocolate Yogurt Mousse
with Whipped Yogurt Cardamom Cream

Mousse is like pudding in its richness and decadence, but unlike pudding, it has an airy texture. In some recipes the cloudlike texture is achieved through whipped egg whites, usually raw, and in others through whipped cream. For this yogurt-based version, I use whipped yogurt sour cream, so you get all of the fluff and indulgence along with the healthy probiotics. As you might have noticed, I'm a fan of spices that are somewhat obscure (at least in regard to most Western recipes). Interestingly, many of them are also from regions of the world where yogurt is a culinary mainstay. For this recipe, I chose cardamom, which adds a subtle nuance to the whipped yogurt cream and pairs nicely with the richness of the chocolate mousse.

Makes 6–8 servings

INGREDIENTS

- 2 teaspoons gelatin or vegetarian option such as agar
- 3 tablespoons cold water
- 2 ounces unsweetened baking chocolate
- ⅛ cup maple syrup
- 1 cup milk
- ¾ cup sugar (I like raw organic)

- 1 teaspoon vanilla extract
- 2 cups yogurt sour cream (page 139)
- ¼ teaspoon salt
- ⅛ teaspoon ground cardamom (you can substitute cinnamon in a pinch)
- Whipped cream or fresh raspberries and mint leaves, for garnish (optional)

STEPS

1. Combine the gelatin and water in a small bowl and set aside to soften.

2. Melt the chocolate in a double boiler over hot water. Add the maple syrup and stir well.

3. Add the milk and set the pan directly on the burner over medium heat. Slowly bring to a boil, stirring constantly. When it reaches a boil, remove the pan from the heat and stir in the softened gelatin, sugar, and vanilla. Place the mixture in a glass bowl and chill in the refrigerator until it begins to thicken, 3 to 4 hours.

4. While the chocolate mixture chills, combine the yogurt sour cream, salt, and cardamom in a bowl and beat until fluffy but not too stiff.

5. When the chocolate mixture is ready, remove from the refrigerator and beat with an electric hand beater or whisk until it is light and fluffy and the color has lightened. Carefully fold in the whipped sour cream, using gentle strokes to keep it light and fluffy.

6. Spoon the mousse into bowls and freeze for 3 hours. Before serving, top with whipped cream or fresh raspberries and a sprig of mint, if desired.

Pumpkin Yogurt Mousse with Candied Ginger

This recipe was an experiment for a Thanksgiving dinner that happily occurred during the writing of this book. I know, a good cook doesn't experiment on guests, but what the heck, sometimes it pays off. I used drained yogurt for the mousse and topped it with whipped yogurt sour cream and candied ginger (it's very easy to make your own candied ginger, but you can also buy it) for a snazzy bit of texture and digestive support. For extra effect, you can garnish the mousse cups with a couple of gingersnap cookies, or for an even prettier, classic British treat, a lacy Florentine cookie.

Most mousse recipes use either whipped cream or raw egg whites to create the characteristic fluffy texture. Because I typically avoid serving raw egg whites to a large group of guests, I used cooked egg white meringue (also known as Italian meringue), which is almost like a creamy, light, and fluffy marshmallow cream.

Makes 6–8 servings

INGREDIENTS

- ½ cup pumpkin purée (canned or fresh)
- 1 cup drained plain yogurt (page 73)
- 4 tablespoons maple syrup, plus 1 teaspoon for the whipped topping, if desired
- ¼ teaspoon ground cinnamon
- ⅛ teaspoon ground cloves
- ⅛ teaspoon ground nutmeg
  Pinch of salt
- ⅓ cup water
- ⅓ cup sugar (I use raw organic)
- 2 egg whites at room temperature
- ¼ teaspoon cream of tartar
- 1 cup cold yogurt sour cream (page 139) or whipped crème fraîche (page 136)

CANDIED GINGER

- 1 (1-inch) piece fresh ginger
- ⅓ cup sugar
- ⅓ cup water

STEPS

1. Combine the pumpkin, yogurt, maple syrup, cinnamon, cloves, nutmeg, and salt in a medium bowl. Stir until well blended. Cover and place in the refrigerator.

2. Combine the water and sugar in a saucepan. Set over medium-high heat and cook, without stirring, until the temperature reaches 238°F (114°C) on a candy thermometer (the "soft ball" stage).

3. While the sugar boils, beat the egg whites in a medium bowl with an electric hand mixer or whisk until foamy. Add the cream of tartar and blend in.

4. When the sugar mixture is ready, immediately drizzle it into the bowl of egg whites with the mixer running. Continue to beat until stiff peaks form and the mixture cools, 8 to 10 minutes.

5. Remove the pumpkin mixture from the refrigerator and, using a rubber spatula, very gently fold in the meringue, blending without beating in order to keep the mixture fluffy.

6. Spoon the mousse into individual serving cups and refrigerate for at least 4 hours to set.

7. While the mousse chills, prepare the whipped yogurt cream: Pour the yogurt sour cream into a bowl and add the maple syrup, if using. Beat with an electric hand mixer or whisk until soft peaks form. The whipped yogurt cream can be made up to a day ahead and stored in the refrigerator.

8. To make the candied ginger, peel the ginger and slice it thinly. Combine the sugar and water in a small saucepan and bring to a low simmer. Add the ginger slices and simmer for 30 to 45 minutes. Remove the ginger slices and cool in a sieve. You can dredge them in more sugar for visual effect, if you like. The liquid left over in the pan makes a great syrup for topping the mousse or using in tea.

9. Just before serving, top each mousse cup with a dollop of the whipped yogurt cream and sprinkle with a few slices of candied ginger (you can chop them smaller, if desired).

Easy Yogurt Crème Brûlée

Crème brûlée is my favorite dessert — one on which I base my final judgment on the restaurant serving it. Deceptively simple, the dish truly reflects the quality of the ingredients and the attention to preparation. When served properly, the custard (the crème part) should be creamy and cool — never warm or hot — while the browned sugar top (the brûlée part) should be a golden to dark brown crystallized crust that you can tap with the edge of your spoon to break into bits. If you have a good broiler in your oven, you can brown the sugar with it, but it's easier, more efficient, and arguably more fun, to use a small butane torch. Prechilling the ramekins in the freezer can help keep the custard cool while you're browning the top.

In order to preserve the yogurt's probiotic bacteria, I make a very thick pudding that is then combined with the cold yogurt. It sets up super fast and is really delicious. To my delight, this recipe was pronounced "the best crème brûlée I've ever had" by a respected chef friend.

Makes 6–8 servings

INGREDIENTS

5 egg yolks

1 tablespoon vanilla extract and/or 1 vanilla bean, split and scraped

⅛ teaspoon ground nutmeg (optional)

Pinch of salt

1½ cups heavy cream

3 tablespoons cornstarch

1 cup cold plain yogurt (page 73)

½ cup granulated sugar (I like raw organic)

1 tablespoon brown sugar

STEPS

1. Combine the egg yolks, vanilla, nutmeg, and salt in a small bowl and whisk until blended.

2. Combine the cream and cornstarch in a small saucepan and whisk until smooth. Set over medium-low heat and cook, whisking constantly, until hot but not boiling, 3 to 4 minutes. Remove from the heat and very slowly drizzle into the egg yolks, whisking constantly. Pour that mixture back into the warm saucepan.

3. Return the pan to medium heat, and stir until the mixture begins to gently boil, 2 to 4 minutes, then reduce heat to low and cook for 1 minute longer. Remove from the heat. It will be an extremely viscous mixture. You may see some separation, but that will disappear as the mixture cools.

4. Place a sieve over a bowl. Work the mixture through the sieve using the back of a spoon to press it through. Blend in the cold yogurt.

5. Pour the custard into ramekins, cover, and chill for 3 to 8 hours.

6. Mix the granulated sugar and brown sugar together, then distribute evenly among the ramekins, sprinkling the sugars on top of the chilled custards. Use a kitchen torch or broiler to quickly brown the sugar into a crust. Rechill if needed to cool the ramekins before serving.

Frozen Yogurt or Kefir Bark

If you're craving frozen yogurt but don't have the equipment to make it, yogurt bark is a satisfying alternative! You'll just need to allow it a bit of time to freeze —2 to 4 hours, depending on your freezer. I've included some sweetener in this recipe, but you can certainly leave it out if you wish. The sky's the limit on toppings! I list some of my favorites, but feel free to experiment.

Makes 1 tray

INGREDIENTS

- 2 cups moderately drained plain yogurt (page 73) or fully drained plain kefir (page 97 or 100)
- 1–2 tablespoons simple syrup (page 213), honey, or agave nectar
- 1 teaspoon vanilla extract (optional; see note)
- Pinch of salt

NOTE: *If you're using the sweet and spicy topping, leave out the vanilla extract.*

Nut and Berry Topping

- ½ cup fresh or frozen berries, such as blueberries, strawberries, and raspberries
- ¼ cup chopped pistachios, walnuts, or almonds

Chocolate Chip and Raisin Topping

- ½ cup semisweet chocolate chips
- ¼ cup golden or brown raisins

Sweet and Spicy Topping

- ½ cup shredded coconut
- ¼ cup chopped dried mango or papaya
- ¼–½ teaspoon hot pepper flakes

STEPS

1. Combine the yogurt, simple syrup, vanilla (if using), and salt in a medium bowl. Mix well.

2. Place a piece of parchment paper on a baking sheet, or use a nonstick sheet. Using a spatula, spread the yogurt mixture over the sheet as evenly as possible. It should be about ¼ inch thick.

3. Evenly sprinkle your topping mix of choice over the yogurt.

4. Freeze until hard, 2 to 4 hours depending on the freezer. Then break into shards. Store the pieces in the freezer in a ziplock bag (remove as much air as possible), and place the bag in a tub to prevent more breakage. If protected from humidity and kept frozen, yogurt bark will last months.

Simple Syrup

Simple syrup, or sugar syrup, is remarkably easy to make. Heat, and sometimes acid, change all or most of the sucrose molecules into glucose and fructose. Its technical name is "invert sugar." You can also buy simple syrup if you don't feel like making it. Use it instead of granulated sugar in any ice cream or frozen yogurt recipe; use about half the amount of sugar that is called for. See the tip on page 204 for why simple syrup helps in frozen desserts.

Makes 1 cup

1 cup sugar (raw sugar adds extra flavor)
1 cup water

Pinch of cream of tartar (an acid source)

Combine the sugar and water in a small saucepan over low heat and bring to a low boil. Add the cream of tartar and let simmer for 20 minutes. During this time, the mixture will lose approximately half its volume as the water simmers away. Cool, then store in the refrigerator.

Yogurt "Cookies"

The following yogurt cookie recipes are based on a simple principle: use the binding power and creaminess of yogurt to meld together different combinations of fruits, nuts, seeds, and other tasty, healthy ingredients, then bake at a low temperature to create a firm, low-sugar, no-wheat, probiotic snack. Once you grasp the ratio of yogurt to dry ingredients, your imagination and pantry are the only limit to your own custom low-bake cookies. These cookies can keep for months in the freezer, but mine seem to never last more than a few days.

Makes 1½–2 dozen

Chocolate Chip, Date, and Almond Yogurt "Cookies"

- ¼ cup almond slivers
- ¼ cup chopped dates
- 2 cups fully drained plain yogurt (page 73)
- ¼ teaspoon salt
- ¼ teaspoon vanilla extract
- ¼ cup mini chocolate chips

Flaxseed, Walnut, and Apricot Yogurt "Cookies"

- ¼ cup walnut halves
- ¼ cup chopped dried apricots
- 2 cups fully drained plain yogurt (page 73)
- ¼ cup flaxseed (optional)
- ¼ teaspoon grated orange zest
- ¼ teaspoon salt

Oatmeal, Raisin, and Cinnamon Yogurt "Cookies"

- ¼ cup rolled oats
- ¼ cup raisins
- 2 cups fully drained plain yogurt (page 73)
- ½ teaspoon ground cinnamon
- ¼ teaspoon salt
- ¼ teaspoon vanilla extract

Mango, Pistachio, and Coconut Yogurt "Cookies"

- ⅛ cup pistachios
- ⅛ cup chopped dried mango
- 2 cups fully drained plain yogurt (page 73)
- ¼ cup shredded coconut
- ¼ teaspoon almond extract
- ¼ teaspoon salt

STEPS

1. Toast the nuts or oats in a dry skillet over medium heat, stirring, until golden brown, about 5 minutes.

Recipe continues on next page

Yogurt "Cookies" *continued*

2. Combine the toasted nuts or oats and the dried fruit in a food processor and finely chop. Add the remaining ingredients (with the exception of chocolate chips, if using) and blend until smooth. Stir in the chocolate chips, if using.

3. Drop the mixture by the tablespoon onto nonstick or parchment-lined dehydrator trays, or cookie sheets if you're drying the cookies in the oven.

4. Dehydrate the cookies at 120°F to 125°F (49°C to 52°C) for 4 hours, or until firm. If you're using an oven, bake at the lowest heat possible for 2 to 3 hours, or until firm. Cool on wire racks. Consume within a few days or freeze.

Get Creative with Yogurt "Cookies"

Every culture that has a long tradition of making yogurt also has a long tradition of drying yogurt to make it more portable and long-lasting (see the sidebar on page 89). When I started experimenting with drying yogurt, I was amazed at how tasty the results were after adding just a few ingredients! It got me started on a slew of variations that were all delicious, gluten-free, full of probiotics, and easy to make. In order to preserve the probiotics, you'll need to dry the yogurt in a dehydrator. You can use your oven if you don't have a dehydrator; the cookies will be done in half the time and have a light golden color, but the higher heat will likely kill most of the probiotic bacteria. They are still a healthy snack, though.

The ingredients in these dried "cookie" recipes can easily be varied to make many different types of treats to fit your family's tastes — and what you have in the cupboard! Just be sure to include a dried fruit for sweetness and some other dry ingredients for texture. None of the recipes contain added sugar, but if you want them to be a bit sweeter, feel free to add the sweetener of your choice.

Yogurt through the Ages

1904	Nobel laureate Elie Metchnikoff urges people to eat yogurt to improve gut health.
Early 1900s	The Battle Creek Sanitarium, a luxurious health spa in Michigan, prescribes yogurt for a healthy diet and for high colonics.
1919	Danone (Dannon) is founded in Spain by Isaac Curasso.
1926	A dairy shop in Athens, Greece, started by Athanassios Filippou and family, starts selling thick yogurt. The family's business will eventually become Fage (fah-yay).
1929	Armenians Rose and Sarkis Colombosian open Colombo Yogurt in Massachusetts. Daniel Curasso opens a Danone plant in France.
1941	Daniel Curasso Dannon opens in the Bronx, New York, in a former Greek yogurt plant.
1947	Dannon introduces fruit-at-the bottom, or sundae-style, yogurt.
1951	Yami Yogurt, based in Los Angeles, takes out an ad in *Life* magazine calling yogurt "nature's nightcap." *The Joy of Cooking* features its first homemade yogurt recipe.
1954	Fage begins distributing yogurt in all of Greece.
1970s	Soy yogurts hit the market.
1970	Nancy's Yogurt, in Oregon, becomes the first yogurt producer to include and advertise probiotics.
1975	Brown Cow, in New York, begins selling the first whole-milk yogurt with cream top.
1977	Dannon launches its famous "Georgians over 100" commercial, linking longevity with yogurt consumption. Yogurt sales increase dramatically.
1982	TCBY, the frozen yogurt chain, goes national. Redwood Hill Farm, in California, introduces the first commercial goat's milk yogurt.
1983	Fage begins exporting yogurt to the rest of Europe.
1988	Lifeway Kefir is founded by Russian immigrants Michael and Ludmila Smolyansky.
1993	Colombo is sold to General Mills.
1994	Old Chatham Sheepherding Company, in New York, introduces the first commercial sheep's milk yogurt.
1998	Fage begins exporting Greek yogurt to the United States.
1999	Yoplait introduces Go-Gurt.
2005	Pinkberry, a frozen yogurt chain, opens its first store.
2007	Fage builds a Greek yogurt plant in the United States. Turkish-Kurdish businessman Hamdi Ulukaya launches the Chobani company in South Edmeston, New York.
2009	Daniel Curasso dies at the age of 103.
2010	After 80 years, General Mills, owner of Colombo, drops that product to focus on Yoplait.
2012	Chobani opens one of the world's largest yogurt-processing plants in Idaho.
2013	Greek yogurt owns 36 percent of the total U.S. national yogurt share.
2017	Annual yogurt sales in the United States are just shy of $9 billion.
2018	Danone USA becomes the world's largest certified B corporation.
2019	Lifeway Kefir introduces a plant-based probiotic fermented beverage.

Acknowledgments

An author is nothing without a great publisher. And a publisher is nothing without a great team. I have been very lucky to have had such teams behind each of the half-dozen books that now bear my name.

Working with three different publishers and six different editors over the past decade has been a delightful education. And that doesn't even begin to count the number of copy editors, proofreaders, designers, salespersons, publicists, and, well, you get the idea!

For this book, I had my first experience working with a professional photographer — having filled that role myself in the past. What a thrill it was to see the vision and creativity of Carmen Troesser bring my recipes and ideas to life in a way that I never could have. The inspired vision of Carolyn Eckert and hard work of production designer Jennie Jepson Smith wove all the words and images together in a beautiful, approachable, and — I hope — inspiring orchestration. Speaking of those words, they were made clearer, more focused, and more concise thanks to my editor, Sarah Guare — thank you! And finally, the multifaceted work of publicist Anastasia Whalen helped to get me and the book out into the world.

It was a thrill to finally work with Storey Publishing — one of the two publishers I sent my first proposal to ten years ago. What a team. What a treat.

References

CHAPTER 2

Plessas, S., C. Nouska, I. Mantzourani, Y. Kourkoutas, A. Alexopoulos, and E. Bezirtzoglou. "Microbiological Exploration of Different Types of Kefir Grains." *Fermentation* 3, no.1 (2016):

Tamime, A. Y. *Probiotic Dairy Products*. Blackwell Publishing, 2007.

CHAPTER 4

Yang, Zhennai, Eine Huttunen, Mikael Staaf, Göran Widmalm, and Heikki Tenhu. "Separation, Purification and Characterisation of Extracellular Polysaccharides Produced by Slime-Forming *Lactococcus Lactis* Ssp. *Cremoris* Strains." *International Dairy Journal* 9, no. 9 (September 1999): 631–38.

CHAPTER 6

Luo, Cheng and Shanggui Deng. "Viili as Fermented Food in Health and Disease Prevention: A Review Study." *Journal of Agricultural Science and Food Technology* 2 (2016): 105–113.

Salminen, Edith. "There Will Be Slime." Nordic Food Lab, April 10, 2014. http://nordicfoodlab.org/blog/2014/3/there-will-be-slime.

Smith, Andrew. *The Oxford Encyclopedia of Food and Drink in America*, vol. 1. Oxford University Press, 2004.

Resources

CULTURES AND SUPPLIES

Belle + Bella
Lexington, MA
www.belleandbella.com
339-970-9888
Culture for dairy or vegan plant milks and YoMagic yogurt maker.

The Cheesemaker
Mequon, WI
www.thecheesemaker.com
414-745-5483
Fresh kefir grains and kits.

Cultures for Health
Morrrisville, NC
www.culturesforhealth.com
Freeze-dried yogurt and kefir cultures, plus many articles and tips.

GEM Cultures
Lakewood, WA
www.gemcultures.com
253-588-2922
Fresh viili culture and fresh kefir grains.

GetCulture
Madison, WI
www.getculture.com
608-268-0462
Cultures, cheesecloth, and miscellaneous supplies.

Lifeway
Morton Grove, IL
www.lifewaykefir.com
847-967-1010
A very nice kefir culture.

Luvele
Walnut, CA
www.luvele.com
A unique yogurt maker with temperature ranges of 96°F to 105°F (36°C to 41°C) for making longer-set (so-called 24-hour yogurt) ferments.

New England Cheesemaking Supply Co.
South Deerfield, MA
www.cheesemaking.com
413-397-2012
A great selection of milk fermentation cultures plus an interactive map for sourcing a variety of milk types.

Savvy Teas and Herbs
Wake Forest, NC
www.savvyteasandherbs.com
Fresh or dried heirloom cultures (not freeze-dried) including a sampler pack of several.

Yemoos Nourishing Cultures
Georgetown, TX
www.yemoos.com
512-819-1561
A wonderful selection, including kefir grains and heirloom cultures.

LEARN MORE
Websites
A Campaign for Real Milk
www.realmilk.com
An invaluable resource for locating raw milk in your locale as well as other information about current raw milk legislation, etc.

Daily Dose of Dairy
www.berryondairy.com

The National Yogurt Association
www.aboutyogurt.com

Russiapedia
https://russiapedia.rt.com/of-russian-origin/kefir
/History of kefir

Books
The Art of Fermentation, Sandor Katz. Chelsea Green Publishing, 2012

Cheese and Fermented Milk, vol. 1, Frank Kosikowski and Vikram Mistry. FV Kosikowki, LLC, 1997

Fermented Milk and Dairy Products, Anil Kumar Puniya. CRC Press, 2015

Mastering Artisan Cheesemaking, Gianaclis Caldwell. Chelsea Green Publishing, 2012

Mastering Basic Cheesemaking, Gianaclis Caldwell. New Society Publishing, 2016

Milk: The Surprising Story of Milk through the Ages, Anne Mendelson. Alfred A. Knopf, 2008

Perfectly Creamy Frozen Yogurt, Nicole Weston. Storey Publishing, 2018

World of the East Vegetarian Cooking, Madhur Jaffrey. Alfred A. Knopf, 1981

Yogurt, Janet Fletcher. Ten Speed Press, 2015

Yogurt Culture, Cheryl Sternman Rule. Houghton Mifflin Harcourt, 2015

PROFILED MAKERS
Bellwether Farms
www.bellwetherfarms.com

GEM Cultures
www.gemcultures.com

Green Valley Creamery
www.greenvalleylactosefree.com

Nancy's Yogurt
www.nancysyogurt.com

Redwood Hill Farm & Creamery
www.redwoodhill.com
www.redwoodhillfarm.org

Metric Conversion Charts

Unless you have finely calibrated measuring equipment, conversions between U.S. and metric measurements will be somewhat inexact. It's important to convert the measurements for all of the ingredients in a recipe to maintain the same proportions as the original.

Weight		
TO CONVERT	**TO**	**MULTIPLY**
ounces	grams	ounces by 28.35
pounds	grams	pounds by 453.5
pounds	kilograms	pounds by 0.45

Temperature		
TO CONVERT	**TO**	
Fahrenheit	Celsius	subtract 32 from Fahrenheit temperature, multiply by 5, then divide by 9

Volume		
TO CONVERT	**TO**	**MULTIPLY**
teaspoons	milliliters	teaspoons by 4.93
tablespoons	milliliters	tablespoons by 14.79
fluid ounces	milliliters	fluid ounces by 29.57
cups	milliliters	cups by 236.59
cups	liters	cups by 0.24
quarts	milliliters	quarts by 946.36
quarts	liters	quarts by 0.946
gallons	liters	gallons by 3.785

Index

Page numbers in *italic* indicate photos or illustrations; numbers in **bold** indicate charts.

Fill Out Your Fermentation Library

with More Books from Storey

by Ricki Carroll

From timeless classics like mozzarella, feta, cheddar, and brie, to sophisticated palate-pleasers such as halloumi, raclette, and gorgonzola, this handbook for the home kitchen covers them all, and includes cheese pairing tips and 50 recipes for cooking with cheese.

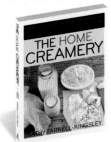

by Kathy Farrell-Kingsley

Make your own dairy products with these easy methods for butter, yogurt, sour cream, and more. Step-by-step instructions are augmented by 75 delicious recipes that use your freshly made dairy, from Apple Coffee Cake with Caramel Glaze to Zucchini Triangles.

by Kirsten K. Shockey and Christopher Shockey

Turn humble beans and grains into a homemade supply of umami-rich, probiotic-packed superfoods. Master the fundamentals of fermenting soybeans and rice, then go beyond the customary ingredients with creative alternatives including quinoa, lentils, oats, and more.

Join the conversation. Share your experience with this book, learn more about Storey Publishing's authors, and read original essays and book excerpts at storey.com. Look for our books wherever quality books are sold or call 800-441-5700.